MIDTOWN SCHOOL OF SCIENCE & TECHNOLOGY

ESTABLISHED 1962

This book belongs to Peter Parker

THE ART OF

MARVEL STUDIOS

SPIDER-MAN™ HOMECOMING

WRITTEN BY

ELENI ROUSSOS

FOREWORD BY

JON WATTS

SLIPCASE ART AND AFTERWORD BY

RYAN MEINERDING

BOOK DESIGN BY

ADAM DEL RE

PROJECT MANGER

ALEX SCHARF

FOR MARVEL PUBLISHING
JEFF YOUNGQUIST, Editor
SARAH SINGER, Editor, Special Projects
JEREMY WEST, Manager, Licensed Publishing
SVEN LARSEN, VP, Licensed Publishing
DAVID GABRIEL, SVP Print, Sales & Marketing
C.B. CEBULSKI, Editor in Chief

FOR MARVEL STUDIOS 2017
KEVIN FEIGE, President
LOUIS D'ESPOSITO, Co-President
VICTORIA ALONSO, Executive Vice President, Visual Effects
JEREMY LATCHAM, SVP, Production & Development
ERIC HAUSERMAN CARROLL, Director, Production & Development
WILL CORONA PILGRIM, Development & Franchise Executive
RYAN POTTER, VP, Business Affairs
ERIKA DENTON, Clearances Director
RANDY McGOWAN, VP, Technical Operations
AXEL SCHARF, Production Asset Manager
MITCH BELL, VP, Physical Production
ALEXIS AUDITORE, Manager, Physical Production

MARVEL STUDIOS' THE INFINITY SAGA - SPIDER-MAN: HOMECOMING - THE ART OF THE MOVIE

ISBN: 9781803368481

First edition: October 2025

10 9 8 7 6 5 4 3 2 1

Published by Titan Books
A division of Titan Publishing Group Ltd
144 Southwark St, London SE1 0UP

www.titanbooks.com

EU RP (for authorities only)
eucomply OÜ Pärnu mnt 139b-14 11317
Talinn, Estonia
hello@eucompliancepartner.com
+3375690241

Did you enjoy this book? We love to hear from our readers. Please e-mail us at: readerfeedback@titanemail.com or write to Reader Feedback at the above address.

To receive advance information, news, competitions, and exclusive offers online, please sign up for the Titan newsletter on our website: www.titanbooks.com

A CIP catalogue record for this title is available from the British Library.

Printed in China

TAMM

MIDTOWN SCHOOL OF SCIENCE & TECHNOLOGY

Student Name PARKER (LAST) PETER (FIRST) B. (MIDDLE)

Parent or Guardian MAY PARKER

Homeroom 14 Locker No. 1184

City and State Queens, New York

	Year	Grade
	10	N/A
	10	A
	10	B+
/ STARK Internship	10	N/A
	10	N/A
	10	C-

FOREWORD 2017

When I started *Spider-Man: Homecoming*, there was no script, no outline, nothing but two simple guiding concepts: 1) Let's make Peter Parker a high school kid, and 2) Let's show Spider-Man doing things we've never seen him do before.

For me, this period is always the most thrilling part of the creative process. There's no plot logic to track, no character motivations to weigh, no production logistics to consider. It's pure visual storytelling. So I set up shop in a cramped little office at Marvel and started to brainstorm with the two most inspiring artists I have ever met: Head of Visual Development Ryan Meinerding and Production Designer Oliver Scholl.

Ryan is the secret weapon of the Marvel Cinematic Universe. His character designs and concept art are unparalleled. When Kevin Feige pitched him the possibility of a Stark-built Spidey-suit and asked what he would want to see it do, Ryan's first thought was to use it as an excuse to make Spider-Man's eyes move. Spider-Man illustrators from day one had played with the shape of Spider-Man's eyes to convey emotion, but it had never been an actual component of the suit. Ryan designed a high-tech irising eye feature that was simultaneously new and classic.

That's Ryan's genius. He finds a way to elevate these comics characters and bring them into the real world while preserving everything about them that we love so much in the first place. I mean, without Ryan, the Vulture would still be an old guy in a winged green leotard and feather boa.

While Ryan and his amazing team were tackling the character designs, Oliver and I were free to come up with style frames for the film. Oliver brings an irresistible amount of enthusiasm to his work, and we had a very lively back-and-forth as we circled around an aesthetic for the film and spitballed potential key scenes—all before a single script page had been written.

I love having those kinds of "Oh, you know what could be cool..." conversations, but this was the first time that they were followed up by gorgeously rendered concept artwork. What would it look like if Spider-Man climbed up the Washington Monument? Bam—here are five incredibly detailed images from Oliver's amazing team. What would it look like if Spidey was sitting on top of the Cyclone on Coney Island? Bam—here's a poster-sized illustration that I want to frame and hang on my wall.

We discovered the visual heart of the film during this process. Massive set-piece ideas like a sliced Staten Island Ferry or a Vulture battle on top of an airplane, as well as smaller character moments like Peter Parker in his bedroom getting busted by Ned. Oliver and his team were an essential part of finding and shaping the story, and I'm eternally thankful for all their brilliant work.

The whole process was addictive. I have to admit, I was pretty sure we were never going to have a scene where Spider-Man rides a dirt bike along the Gowanus Canal, but I couldn't resist pitching it to the concept artists. I wanted to see it. And now you can, too.

To Ryan and Oliver—thank you so much from the bottom of my heart. I couldn't have done it without you.

Jon Watts

JON WATTS

WORLD BEAT

Congratulations, Midtown Tigers, on a fantastic year! It was filled with ups and downs, but we somehow managed to keep a smile on Principal Morita's face. Here are just some of the highlights:

This year saw the arrival of Spider-Man in our friendly neighborhood. I'm sure we can all agree how excited we are about our local hero!

"Part of what makes Spider-Man so great in the comics is his ability to exist in this broader world of super heroes. Previously in the fi lms, there was no one else in the universe. So Spider-Man had to do everything himself. And in this world, we're setting up this notion that Tony Stark is recruiting young Peter into the Avengers. He can now have a little of Tony Stark's ingenuity. Maybe Tony Stark can help him out. Maybe Tony Stark can give him some pointers. It's not like Tony Stark's going to come in and do everything. But there can now be some collaboration, which is kind of cool and something that's never been done, and can allow us to justify some of the tech that exists in the Spider-Man suit that maybe a 15-year-old kid wouldn't necessarily have access to—even if he is the biggest genius in the world."

— **Executive Producer Jeremy Latcham**

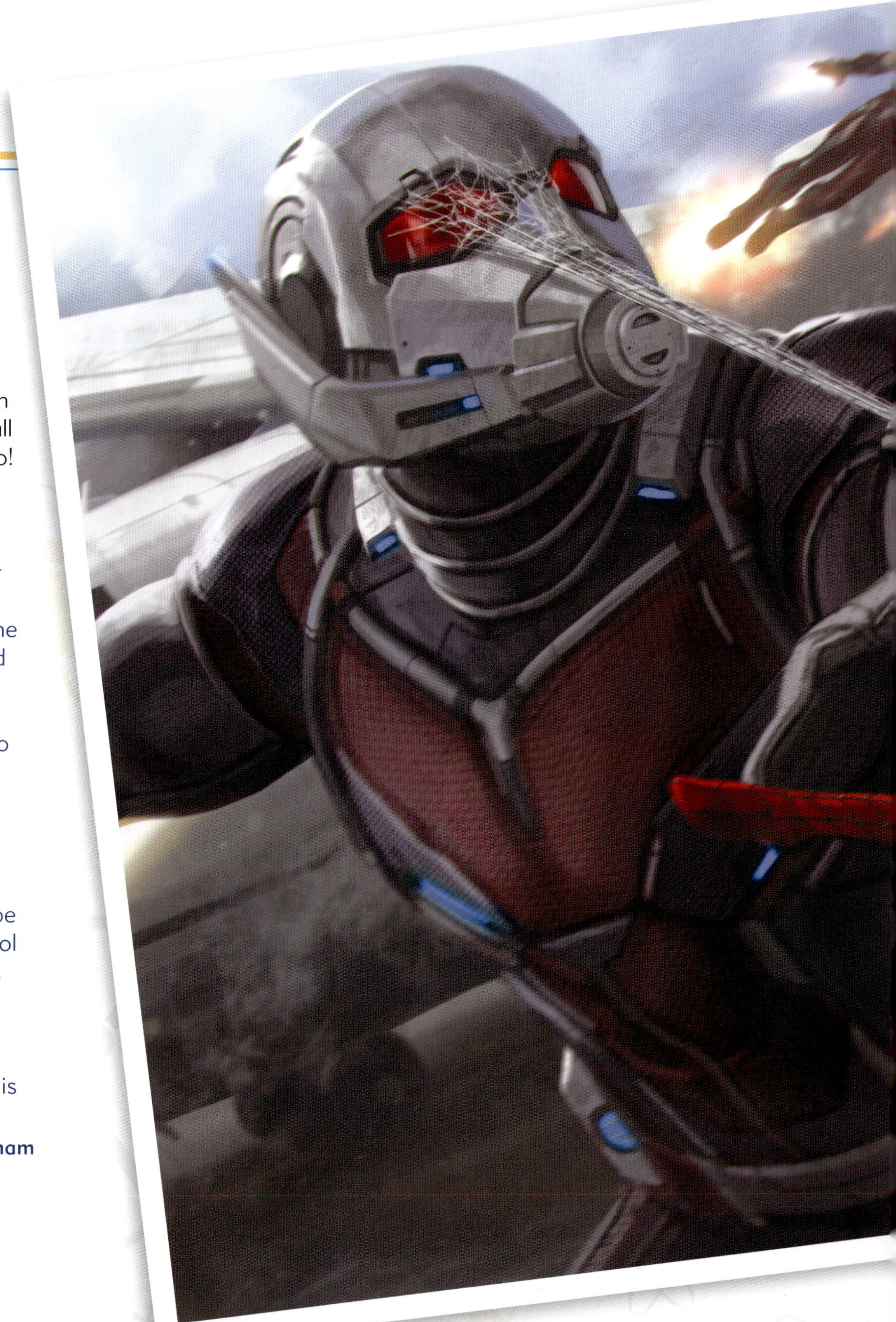

PARK |

"I like the idea of just telling the story at Peter's level, from Peter's perspective. So the audience is feeling and seeing and experiencing everything with Peter as it's happening. I love the idea of three movies that all take place in high school—sophomore year, junior year, senior year—because then we can really spend some time watching a kid's growth in the same way. The other movies really just sort of jumped ahead, like now he's ready to be a super hero. I think that's a much more complicated and rich journey to get to that point. And that's what I want to really, really study."

— Director Jon Watts

Spider-Man was thrust into the spotlight after joining #TeamIronMan to fight #TeamCap. He made a strong showing and did our city proud! Now, Spidey's fighting the good fight back on his home turf—and proving that it takes more to be a hero than a flashy suit and the latest tech.

We were only in elementary school when Tony Stark announced himself as Iron Man; since then, the Avengers have been ever-present in our lives, even saving our city from aliens in the Battle of New York. It's such a thrill to see our favorite web-head meet them all—and learn from the greats!

"It's so important to Spidey that he doesn't have any of all that fancy stuff they all have with houses and cars and gods and things. But then it was just true that the idea of putting him up against a world where everybody had everything and he had nothing was a whole new way of telling his story."

— **Producer Amy Pascal**

Midtown's Academic Decathlon team—led by senior Liz Allan—provided another one of the year's highlights by bringing home a national championship following an intense competition in our nation's capital. The team faced a harrowing ordeal while visiting the

"It's really about a kid trying to deal with doing his homework, asking the girl to the dance, being late for school—but also trying to save New York from this crazy villain. We really get to explore a kid having fun and enjoying himself, which often isn't the case with super heroes. Often being a super hero is a burden. But right now, for Peter, it is the best thing that could possibly have happened to him."

— **Tom Holland**

PARK |

FUENTEBELLA

Washington Monument, but tragedy turned to triumph as Spider-Man saved the day.

We love our friendly neighborhood Spider-Man!

"This film is going to take Spider-Man to places and to locations out of New York City—in areas we haven't seen him fight before, we haven't seen him live in before—all because that's going to add a freshness to it. And Spider-Man didn't always just stay in New York City in the comics. He can go to the outer boroughs. He can go to other states. He takes a trip down to Washington, D.C.—so we can get these different flavors to Spider-Man, which existed in the books before."

— **Producer and Marvel Studios President Kevin Feige**

Putting together this retrospective with the rest of the yearbook committee was truly a labor of love. I hope you find inspiration in the concept art and photography to follow, along with quotes from various students and faculty. If these are the moments that shape the direction of the future, I know it's in good hands.

Go get 'em, Spidey!

Betty Brant
Editor in Chief

FIRST PERIOD

HOMEROOM

Midtown School of Science and Technology—THERE'S A PLACE HERE FOR EVERYONE! For those lucky enough to attend, Midtown provides the perfect springboard to help students discover their best selves. It is within these walls that we truly start to explore who we are as people and realize our full potential. The challenges we face here, although seemingly difficult to overcome in the moment, will make us stronger in the future.

"One of the great things about Spider-Man in the comics is the importance of his everyday life in his adventures. Spider-Man comics are always about how Peter Parker's life is affecting being Spider-Man and vice versa. And when you really look at the backdrop of high school, what you have is all that great soap-opera stuff, like what girl does Peter have a crush on this week? Does that girl like somebody else? Who's interested in who? And did he get his homework in on time, or was he out crimefighting too late? And I think the backdrop of high school gives a lot of dramatic opportunities there that make it feel different than the other super-hero movies that are out right now."

— Co-Producer Eric Carroll

PERCEPTION NYC

KUNITAKE

TAMM

POUI

TAMM

MIDTOWN SCHOOL OF SCIENCE & TECHNOLOGY

KALABA |

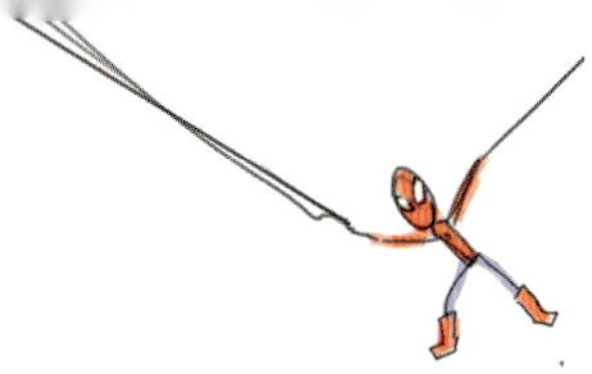

WE'VE GOT SPIRIT, YES WE DO! What better way to show your Midtown Tiger pride than by sporting our school colors? Our P.E. classes, cheerleading squad, and various sports teams all rocked the blue and gold this year—looking just as stylish as ever!

"The original school colors were teal and gold. But teal looks so horrible on most skin tones, and it makes people look ill, so we decided to change it. We came up with a perfect shade of blue to replace the teal."
— Costume Designer Louise Frogley

CORDELLA

SECOND PERIOD

WEB DESIGN

One of Midtown's most popular classes is Web Design. Students find inspiration in previous iterations in comic books, television, cinema, and other media, expanding on what has gone before to make it their own. The web is a revolution—the way of the future!

> Every challenge with an important character has always felt very heavy. But Spidey is additionally challenging because his costume is so simple that if you're going to make a mistake, it is going to be very apparent. And it's hard because of the simplicity as well. There are a limited amount of opportunities to change it in a way that can make it slightly new, but still have it be classic.
>
> I think the notion of looking at the previous movie suits and understanding how much everyone has enjoyed and loved those costumes, if there is going to be a greater weight to it, it is going to be because of that. I wouldn't say that the pressure is more, it just feels like there's so much more at risk.
>
> **— Head of Visual Development Ryan Meinerding**

MEINERDING

SPIDER-MAN

PETER PARKER

Arguably no super-hero design is more iconic than that of Spider-Man. Children have doodled his costume, web patterns, and *thwips* in the margins of notebooks for decades. But what happens when you ask some of the world's most talented artists to honor the past while simultaneously reimagining everyone's favorite web-slinger for new generations?

"The Spider-Man costume is probably, with no exaggeration, one of the best graphic-designed elements in the history of graphic design. It is an unbelievably well-done image. I see kids come in, and babies who can't speak who come into our office and gravitate over to the Spider-Man drawing, the Spider-Man toy, the Spider-Man character. These kids focus in. So when you sit down to make a Spider-Man movie, you don't go, 'How are we going to change the most perfect piece of graphic design in the history of the medium?' You sit and go, 'How can we pull that to the surface in a different way, in a more unique way—while in certain ways staying more true to the conceit of the image than ever before, while at the same time taking it places that you haven't seen in the other films."

— Producer and Marvel Studios President Kevin Feige

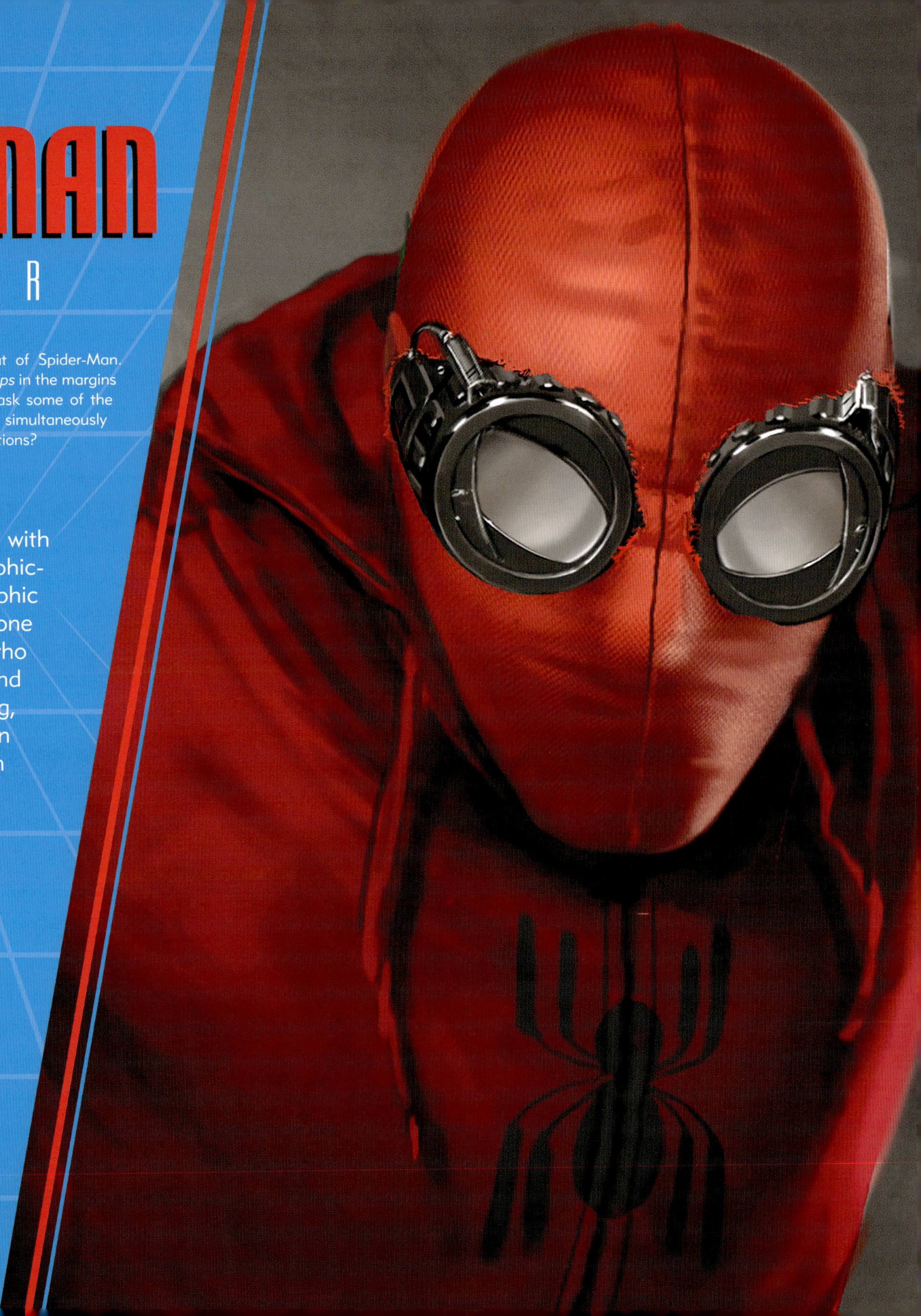

MEINERDING

Every super hero has to start somewhere, and that includes a first costume. Not only is this version entirely plausible for a high-school student to have created on his own, but this Spider-Man's homemade suit also showcases a new color palette for the web-slinger.

"There are runs in the comics where the blue on Spidey's suit is actually a lighter blue than the value of the red, and I just always loved that concept. The homemade suit was really based on trying to find a way of getting that color scheme with the powder blue and a really strong red, and using a Todd McFarlane spider on the chest. It just felt like a more innocent version of Spider-Man. And since Tom [Holland] was going to play an actual high-school kid, it made sense having a suit that has an almost childlike innocence to it."
–Ryan Meinerding

MEINERDING

AGE 14
AGE 11
AGE 9
AGE 8
AGE 6
Peter

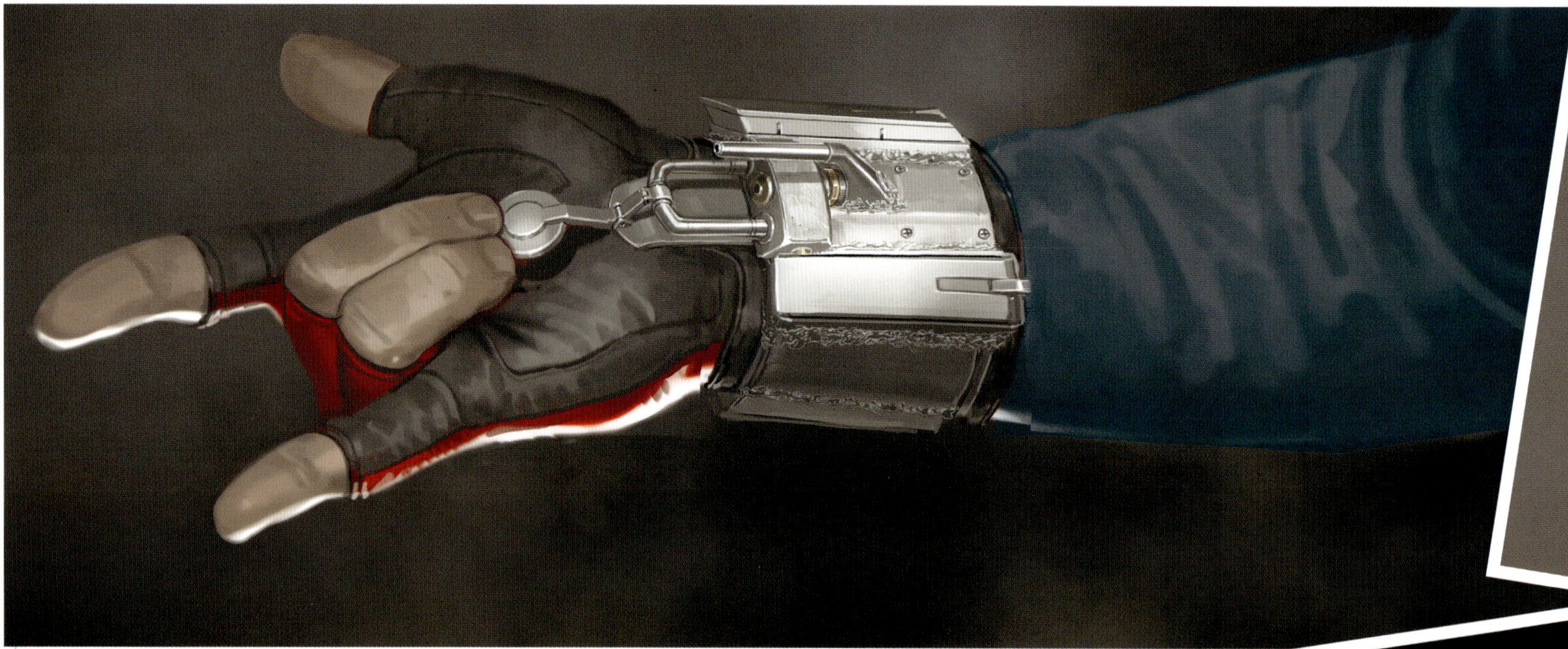

MEINERDING

"When I was a kid, I would get those drawings that would show the cutaways of the suit and show what Spider-Man's actual web-shooter looked like, and the stuff in the comics was always silver and always had a pretty prominent trigger button. In the previous movies, I always wished there was more of that type of exploration. I also thought an external web-shooter could be fun because you could see him refilling cartridges, like it could become part of the action. It wouldn't just be this thing that he was so cool that his webs would just happen without you seeing it."

–Ryan Meinerding

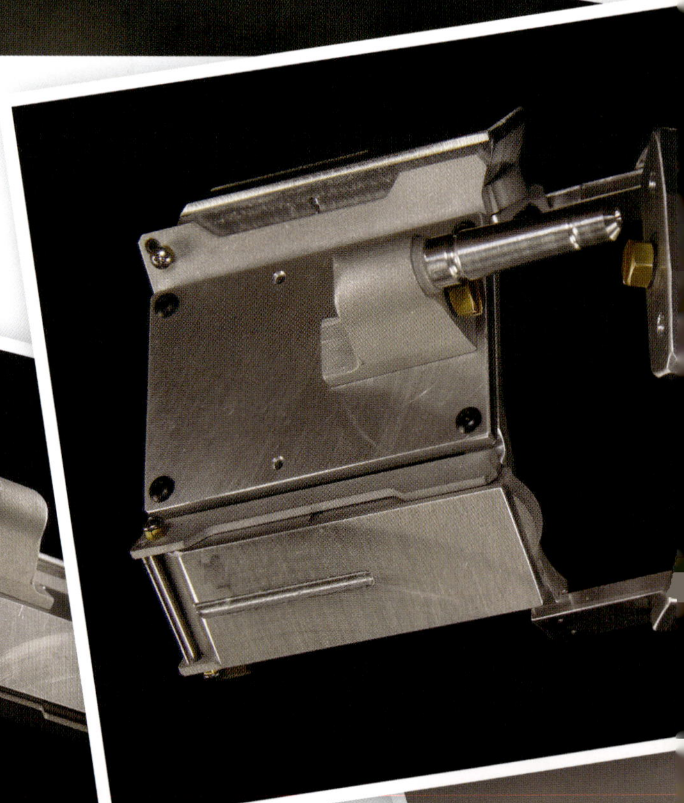

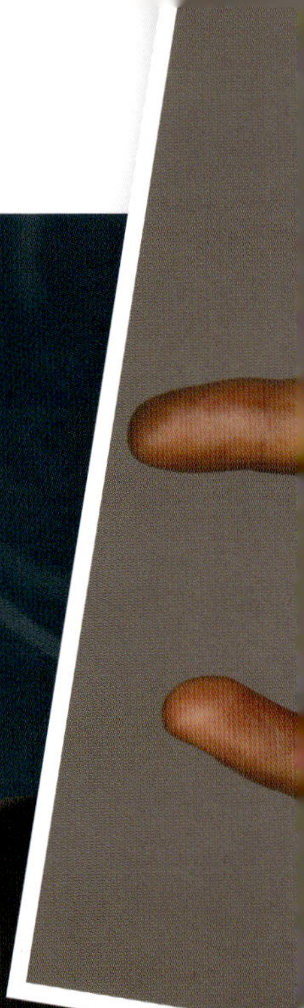

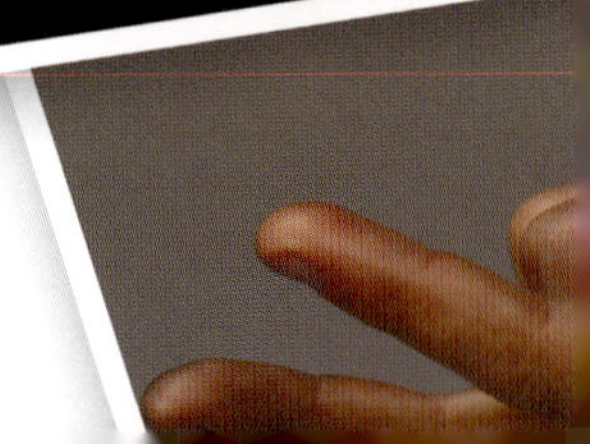

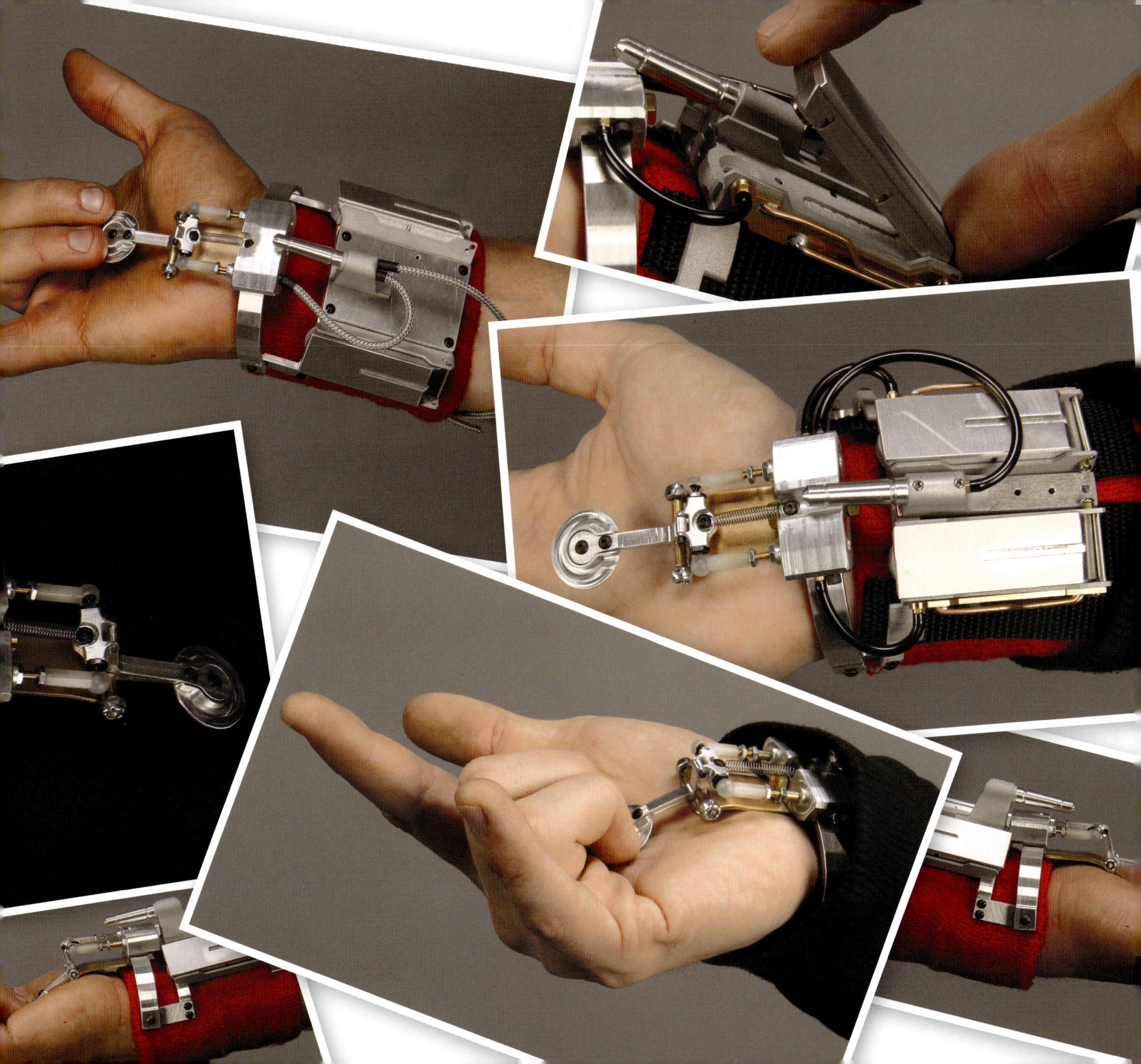

MEINERDING

| HERMAN

FUENTEBELLA

LANG

PARK | MEINERDING

In contrast to Spidey's makeshift suit, the Stark-made Spider-Man costume is a high-tech wonder. Having a costume created by Tony Stark helps explain not only its degree of technological integration, but also other surface-level design elements far too sophisticated to have sprung from a 15-year-old's mind.

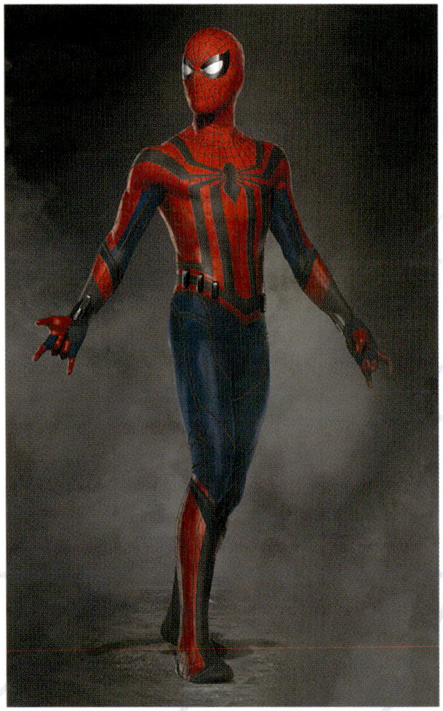

MEINERDING

"A lot of the stuff up front is, 'How do we make this different from the previous versions? If Tony Stark designed this suit, let's bring in some of the design detailing that Tony would have put into it, like what he had already put into Captain America's costume, and then let the spider be a little bit more technologically driven."

–Ryan Meinerding

MEINERDING

MEINERDING

"The first version I had done was a red and black suit, with a different kind of detailing on the chest. If you look back at Steve Ditko's original run, because so much of the dark areas are actually black with blue highlighting, you could argue that the suit is actually red and black, which is one of the things we were trying to pitch. But there is also the general notion in the public of who Spider-Man is, and it's not red and black."

-Ryan Meinerding

MEINERDING

FUENTEBELLA

"One of the things we run through in terms of where to come up with design ideas is if there is a reason for something—is there a purpose or practical cause for a suit to be a certain way."
–Ryan Meinerding

MEINERDING

MEINERDING

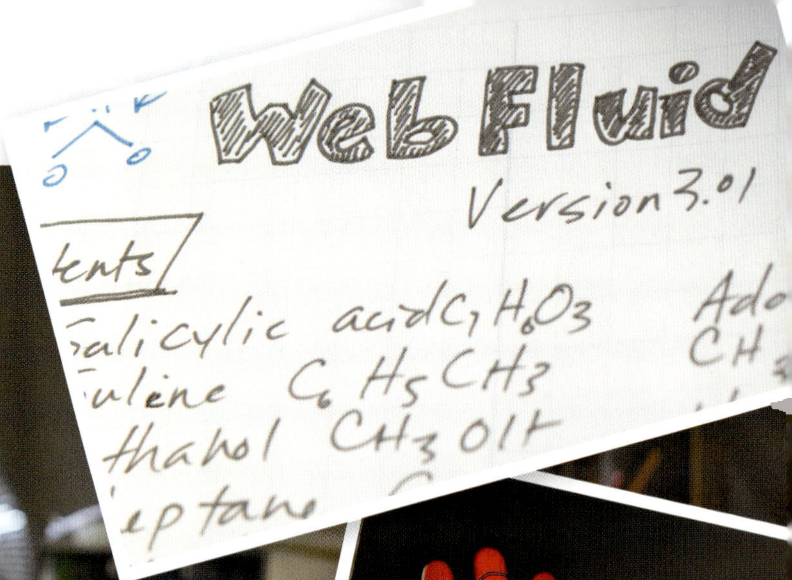
Web Fluid
Version 3.01

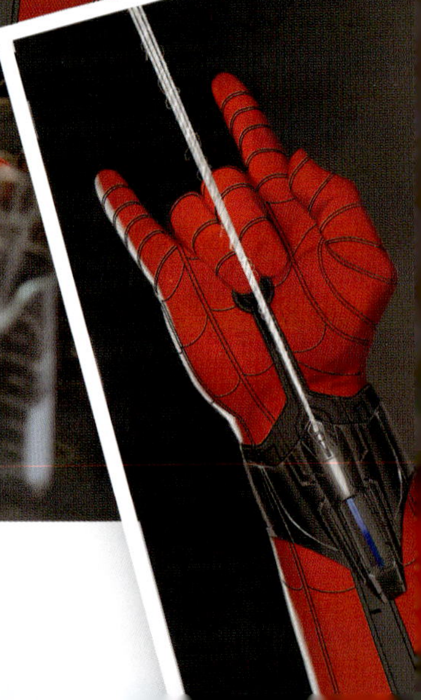

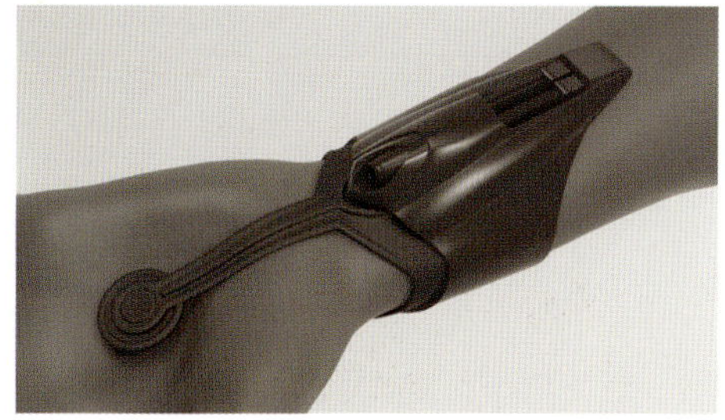

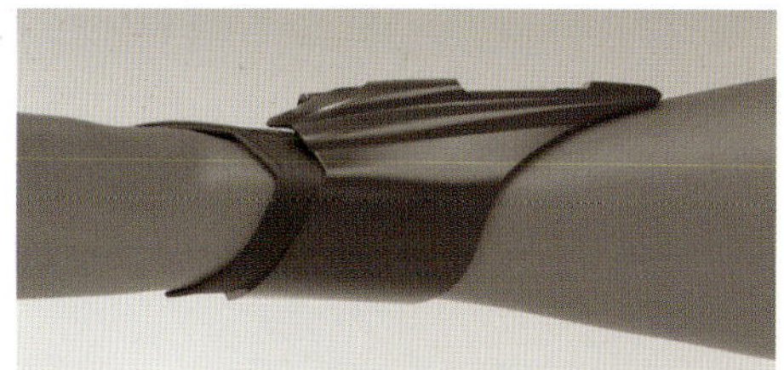

Spider-Man's web-fluid vials had to be both functional and aesthetically pleasing.

"When we started, we made everything opaque—and that had a really nice, clean look to it—but you couldn't see how the web shooters worked. The team wanted the cartridges to be clear so you could see the inside. They didn't want anything encased. That way, the audience would be able to see how the shooters worked: The two fluids would mix and catalyze and turn into web. Plus, you would need them to be clear from a functional standpoint to know if they were full or not."
-Concept Artist John Eaves

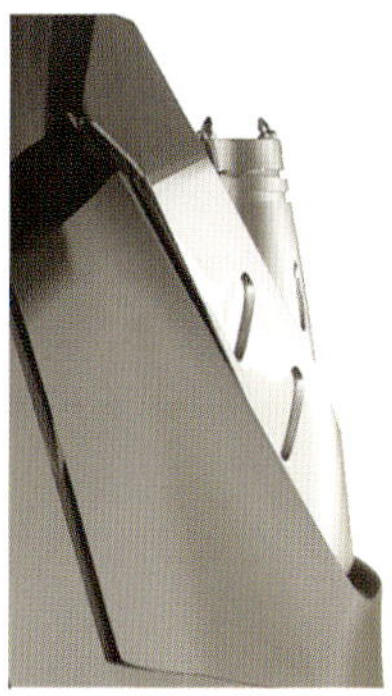

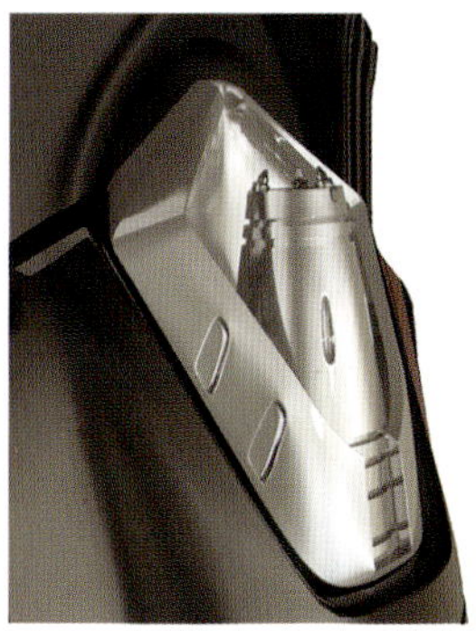

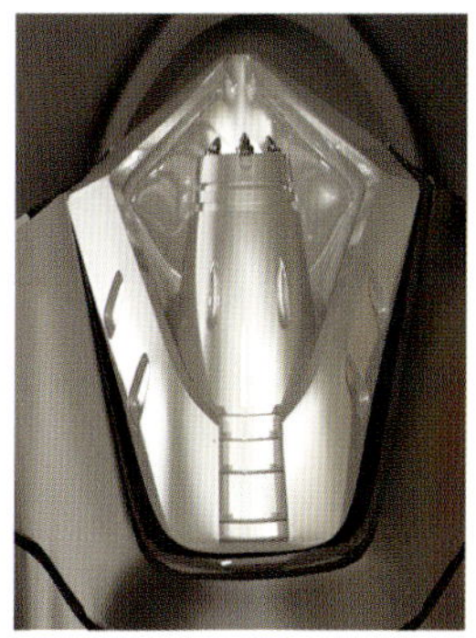

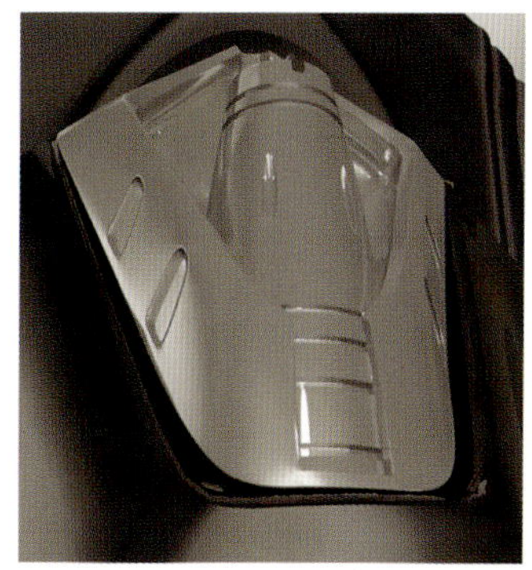

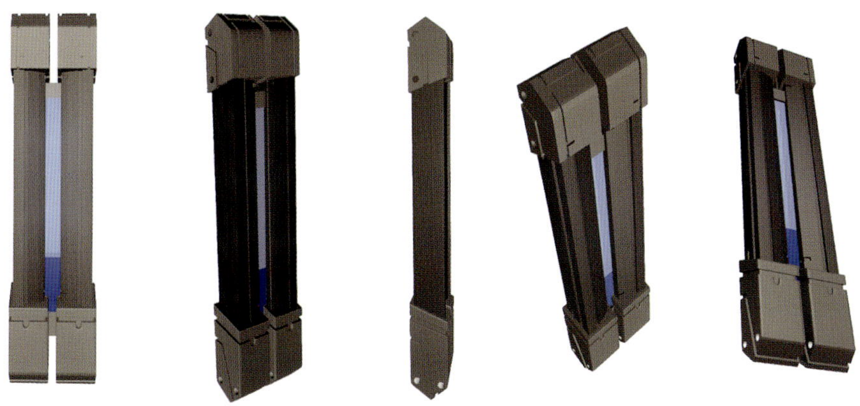

MEINERDING | EAVES

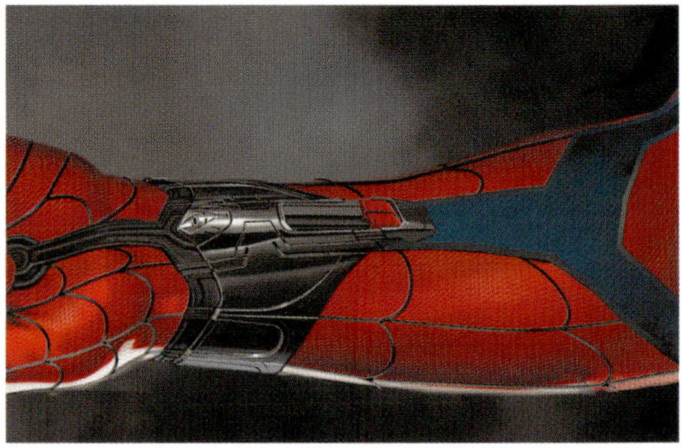
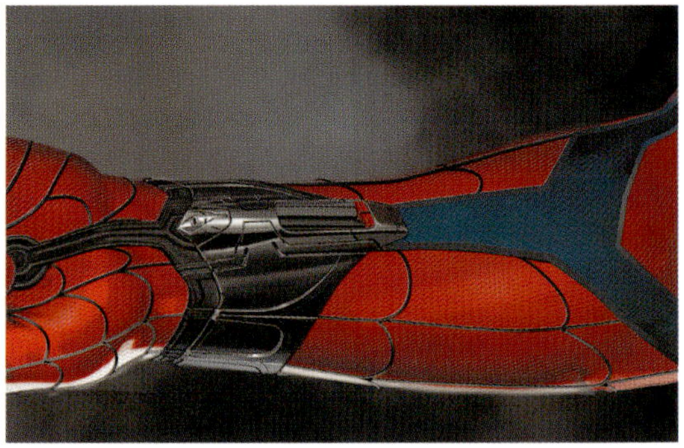
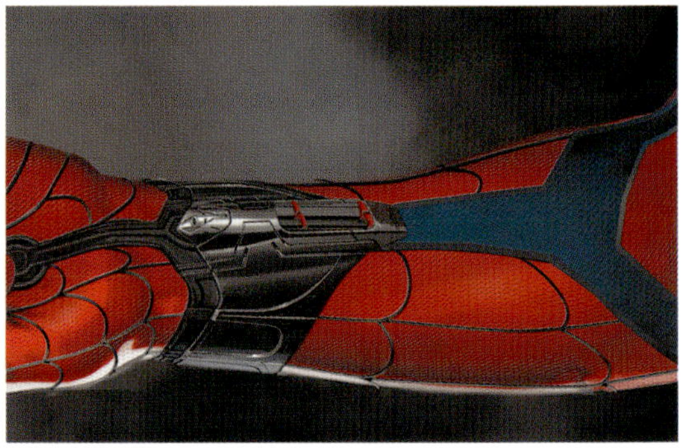
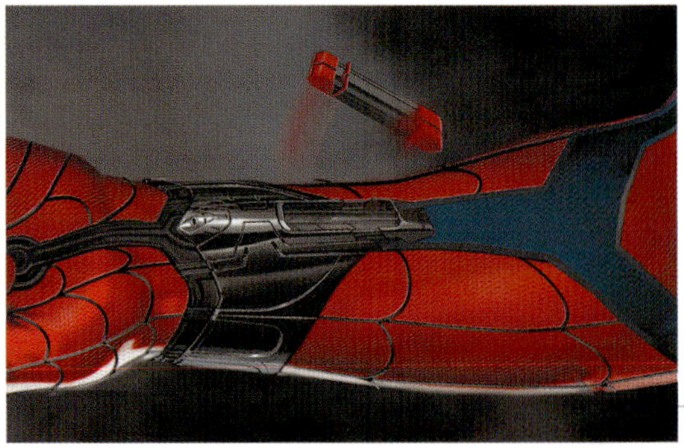

FUENTEBELLA

"How does he do that? How does he get up on that building? How does he resist a pull? How does he flip over? How does he walk when he's going from A to B and he doesn't know what power he's embodying as he's using it? What is the reaction time before, 'Oh, wow, I just did a very cool thing?' I mean, after all, he's a kid."
— Executive Producer Victoria Alonso

MEINERDING

Unlike previous on-screen versions, this Spider-Man can run out of webbing—his web-shooters are not filled with an unlimited supply.

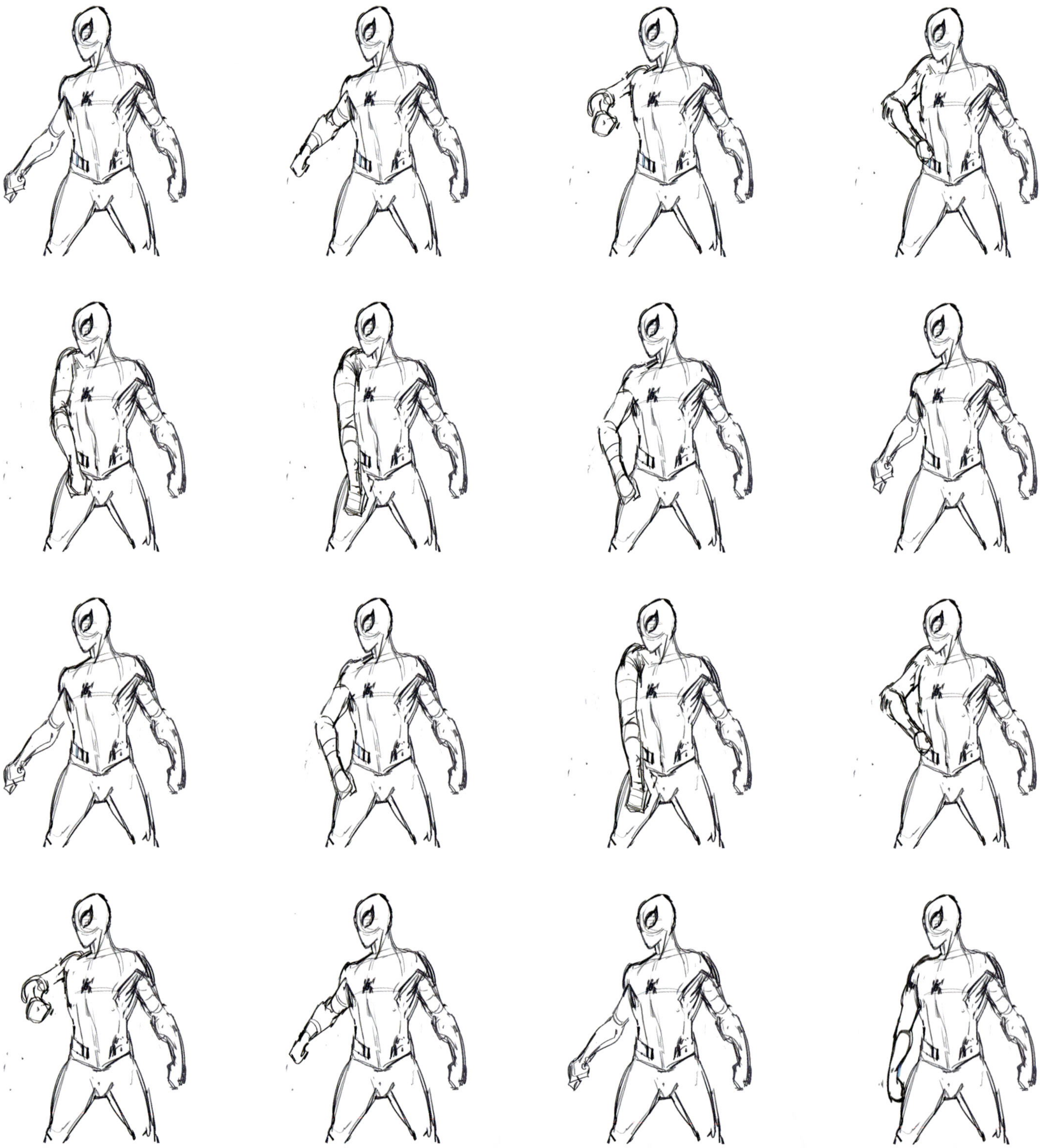

"We wanted a way to show the audience how he would reload his web cartridges fast and with efficiency—to try to make it feel like it is a new, high-tech way of reloading his web-shooters, but not make it so otherworldly or too complex that the audience won't get it. It needs to make sense. These sketches are fun to do—to come up with something that is new and innovative, but still something that feels like what Spider-Man is."
— Concept Artist Rodney Fuentebella

| FUENTEBELLA

| PREVIOUS MEINDERING

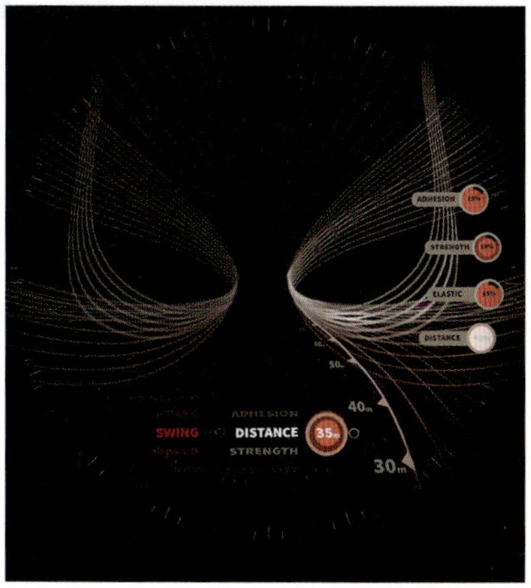

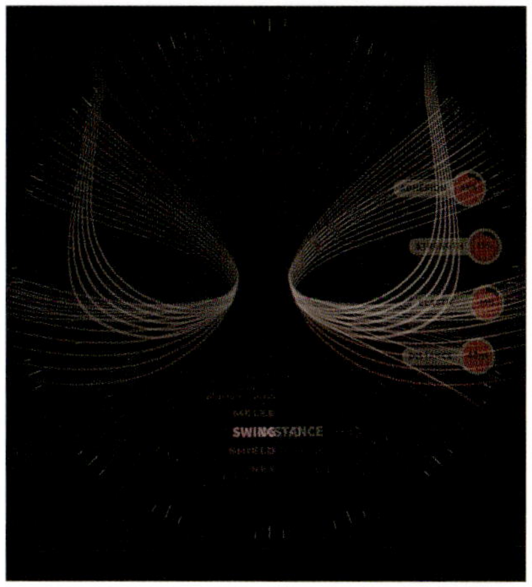

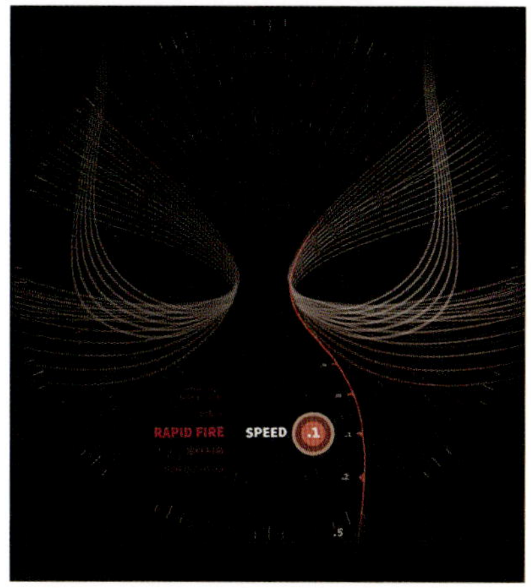

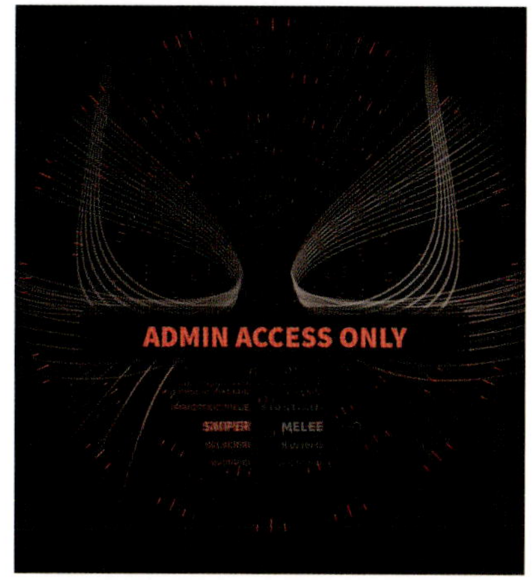

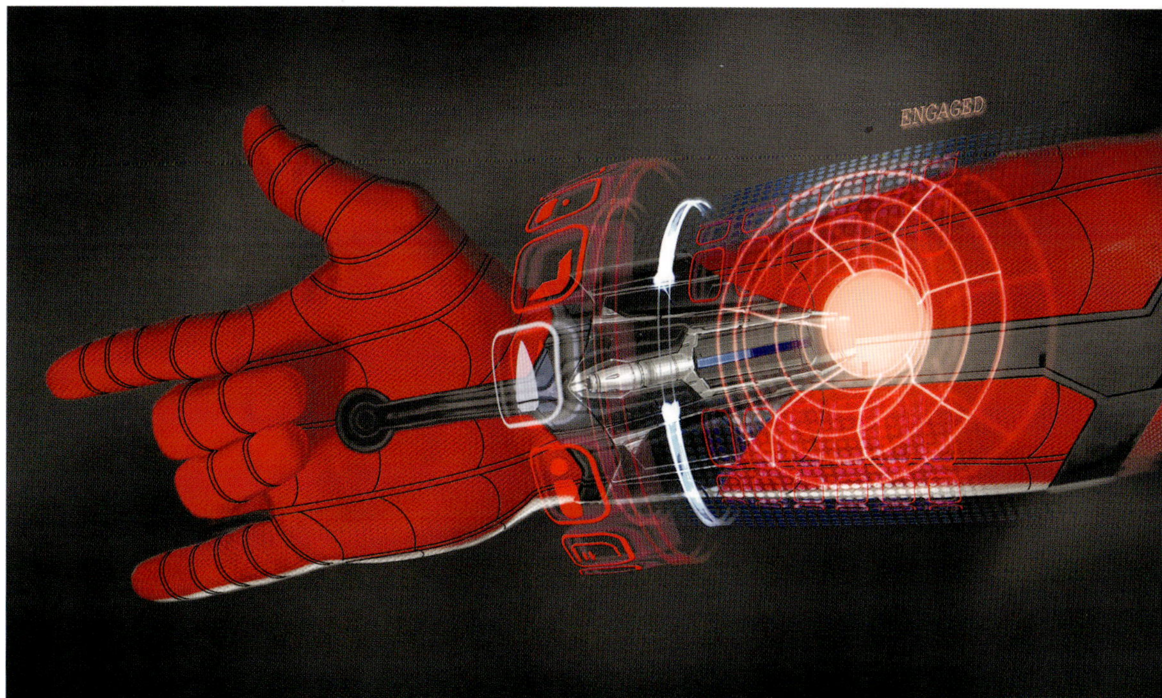

| FUENTEBELLA

"We have this great opportunity because this suit has been designed by Tony Stark, so it is more high-tech than any suits that we've seen before. It can do more than we've ever seen in any of the movies, and maybe more than even Peter realizes."
— Director Jon Watts

NIZZI

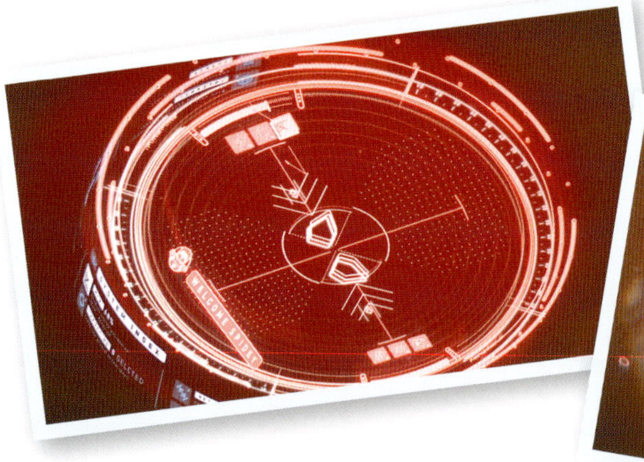

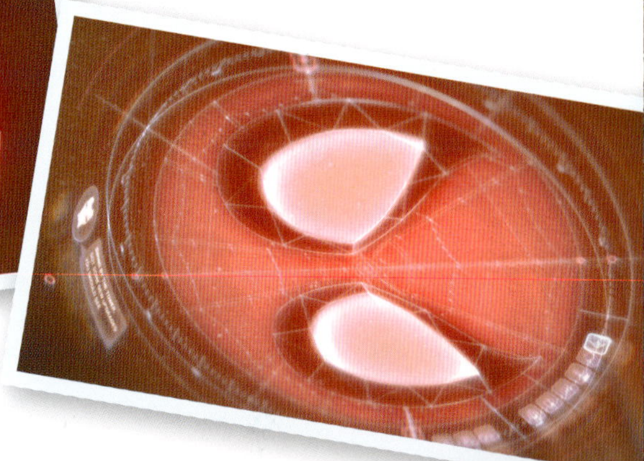

NIZZI

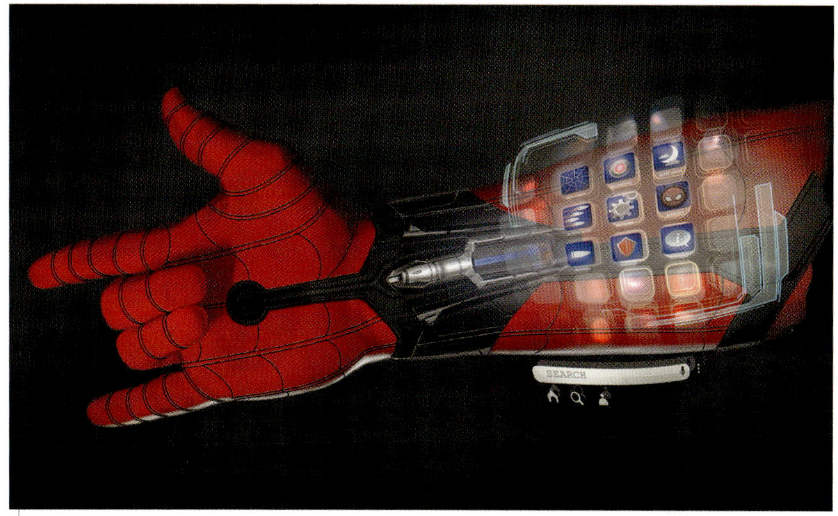

MEINERDING & FUENTEBELLA

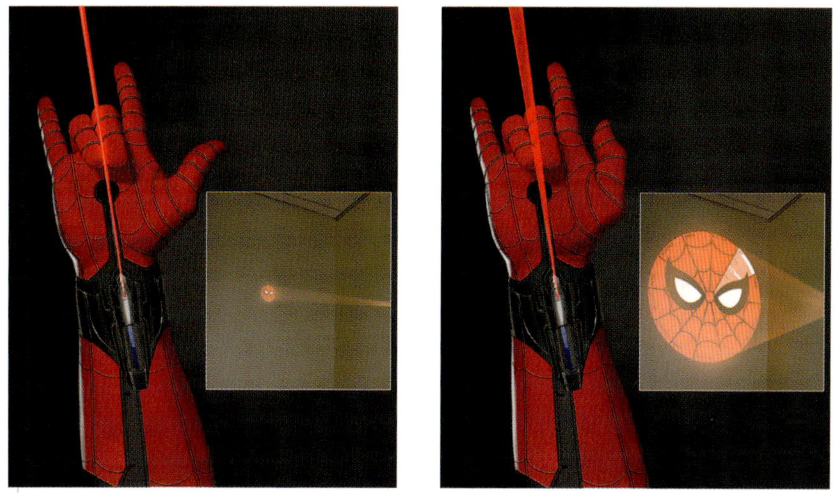

MEINERDING

"We've always had to believe that Peter Parker would've invented this suit by sewing it on a sewing machine, and we just kind of went with it. Now we don't have to do that anymore. Now Tony Stark's actually made him a suit that has all kinds of things and all kinds of devices that Peter's going to discover."
— Producer Amy Pascal

As with any piece of technology, there's a chance Spider-Man's smart costume could stop working, experience a glitch, or stall out—issues Peter never would have experienced when his suit was made of cloth.

"For the light-up suits, we wanted to come up with an idea of different ways of how to show how the suit is malfunctioning. I wanted to show that if the suit is having issues and going crazy, there could be some LED lights going off or something similar to visually let Peter know something was going wrong with the suit. Basically, if it goes off, something isn't going well at all."

– Rodney Fuentebella

FUENTEBELLA

When Steve Ditko designed Spider-Man for his comic-book debut in 1962's *Amazing Fantasy #15*, he gave him what are now known as web-wings. While they appear periodically in the comics, this is the first time the web-wings will be seen on film.

FUENTEBELLA

"We wanted to try and make it feel high-tech. We looked at the comics for inspiration as well as modern winged suits, squirrel suits, and even sailboats to try and get an idea of the complexity of the material, but at the same time the simplicity of the shapes. I feel it is one of those important parts of Spidey that we needed to make sure fit with the overall design of the costume."
– Rodney Fuentebella

MANDRADJIEV

FUENTEBELLA

NIZZI

"When a kid plays with something for the first time, things don't just come exactly right. That is kind of what these suit gags with Spidey are. The suit inflating, or him being propelled, or him getting caught in the web—the suit could function in the right context, he just isn't doing it correctly."
– Rodney Fuentebella

FUENTEBELLA

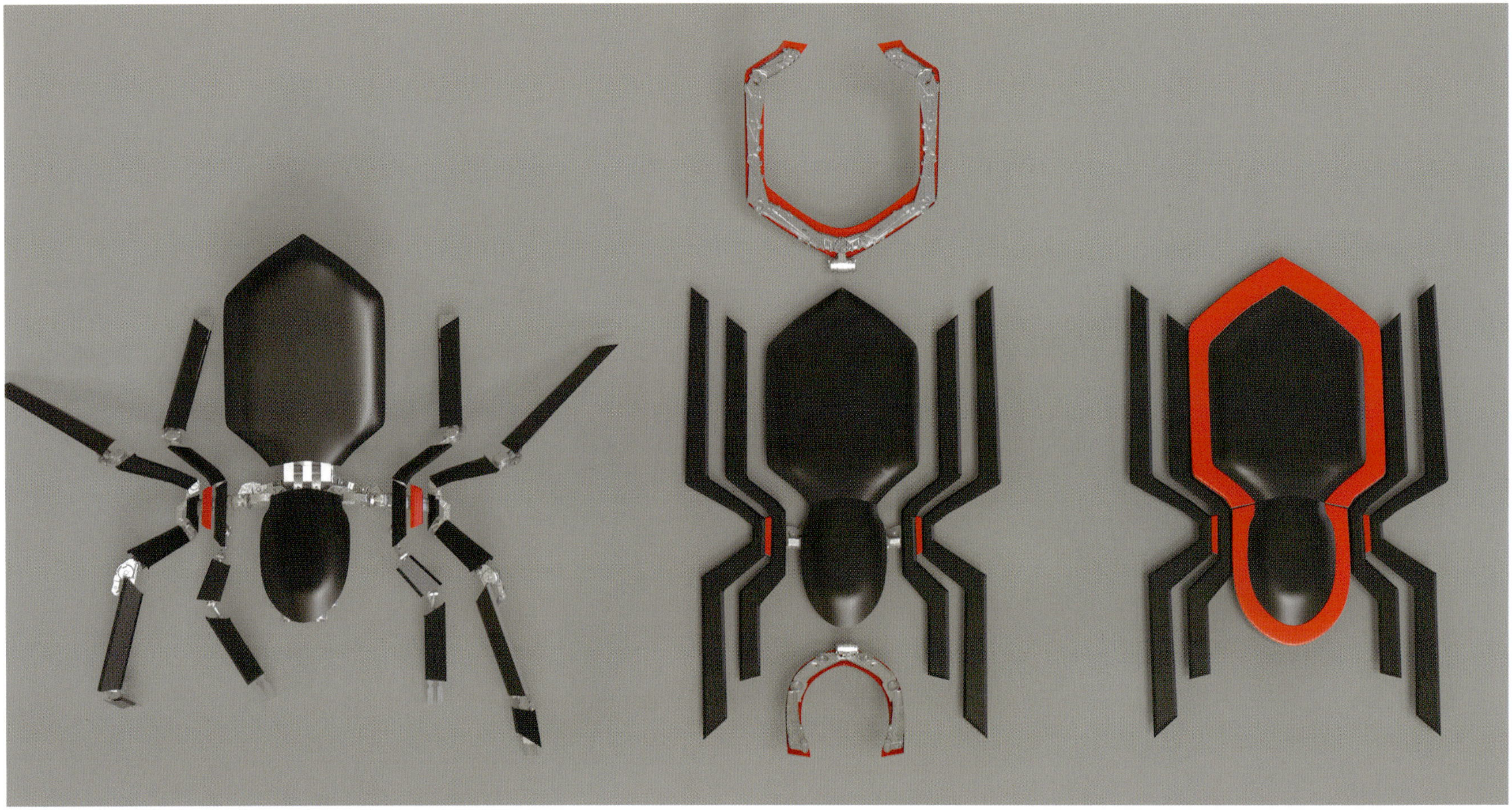

NIZZI

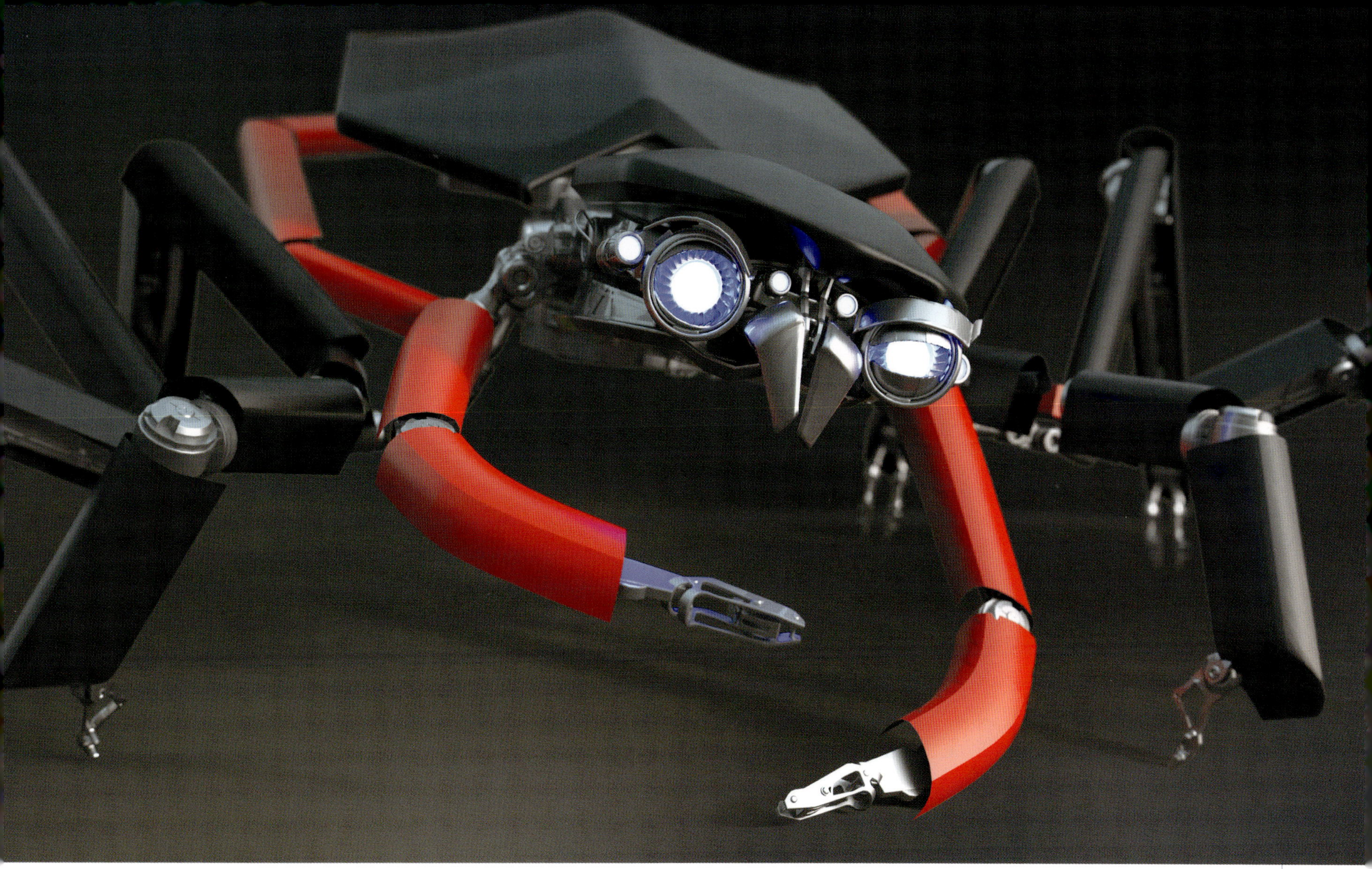

NIZZI

Perhaps the most prominent aspect of Spider-Man's suit—right in front of fans' faces for decades—inspired one of the new ideas in *Spider-Man: Homecoming.*

"We all talked about the suit being designed by Stark, and one of the running gags would be that it would keep doing these things that he didn't know about, and have these surprise abilities. The idea of the Spider on the chest being a drone that could pop out was one of them. So they really wanted to have it be something that could fly, and wanted it to be like a little buddy. We had to try to find that line of the drone is a robot but has his own AI and determine how much personality to give him, but the overall idea made for a pretty interesting design. It almost gives purpose for the symbol being there. It's pretty ingenious."

– Concept Artist Josh Nizzi

MEINERDING

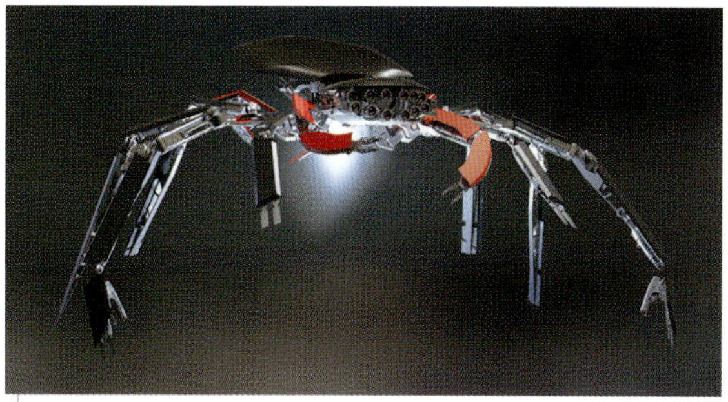

NIZZI

THIRD PERIOD

SHOP CLASS

Thomas Edison invented the phonograph. Nikola Tesla harnessed the power of alternating current. What future inventions will Midtown students create? Shop Class provides us with hands-on experience manipulating unfamiliar materials—sometimes whatever scraps we can scrounge up—to create new and exciting contraptions!

> "I think that your everyday criminal is starting to feel outgunned, outmanned, and outflanked. He can't compete. How do you compete in a world with Iron Man? When Falcon can show up, when War Machine can show up, when Vision can show up? As a street-level criminal, you probably start to feel pretty useless. Well, what if I could get some of that stuff that those guys have? What if those guys inspired me to take my criminality up a level, to take my villainy up a level, or to actually start becoming a bad dude and start doing these crazy things?"
>
> **— Executive Producer Jeremy Latcham**

PUI

MICHLAP

PUI

PUI

PUI

Aliens have attacked New York City, Helicarriers have fallen from the sky, and entire cities have been ripped from their foundations. The world has changed, and so have the rules. The petty crimes committed by thieves, thugs, and common criminals pale in comparison to the massive plots of global powers and celestial super-beings. More down-to-earth villains must adjust to this new landscape. Their plans need to be more elaborate, their solutions more creative, and their weapons infinitely more sophisticated.

"I really like the idea that we're going to start with villains with ground-level problems that you can relate to. It's not about world domination. It's not about some crazy revenge plot. It's more just about not having enough money to get by, not feeling disrespected, and really wanting to have a place in the world even though these super heroes exist."
— Director Jon Watts

AVERY

TAMM

BUOEN

KUNITAKE

TAMM

BUOEN

"As always, we start from what the story calls for, and since Toomes and Mason salvaged primarily from the Battle of New York, a lot of our tech was based on Chitauri stuff. [Production Designer] Oliver [Scholl] and I had many discussions about the sources of the weaponry with Jon [Watts] and our Marvel team. The Marvel guys have an encyclopedic knowledge of not only the past Marvel films, but also the films they are planning in the future, so they were our main guides."

– Property Master Kirk Corwin

TAMM

The villains in *Spider-Man: Homecoming* manipulate everything from alien tech to sub-Ultrons to old Iron Man parts to create their inventions. Property Master Kirk Corwin had the full range of past MCU films at his disposal to find inspiration for the various tools and weaponry used by the bad guys.

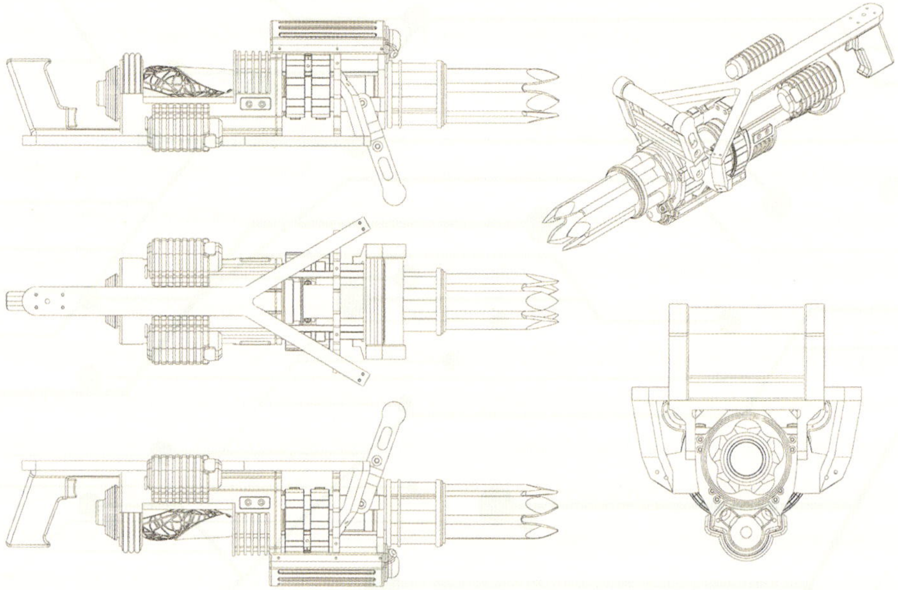

"The team wanted existing guns as the base. We chose a select group of rifles to use and added Chitauri tech to it—that gold and blue Chitauri stuff from Marvel's The Avengers with organic sheeting. That added the sci-fi element gives the sense of a kind of mystical power source—something that could turn a human-made invention like a gun into something a little bit more powerful. We had to keep that gold color between what would be manmade and what would be Chitauri, so we used darker weapons. They really wanted a high contrast between the two materials."
- Concept Artist John Eaves

PREVIOUS **KUNITAKE**

EAVES

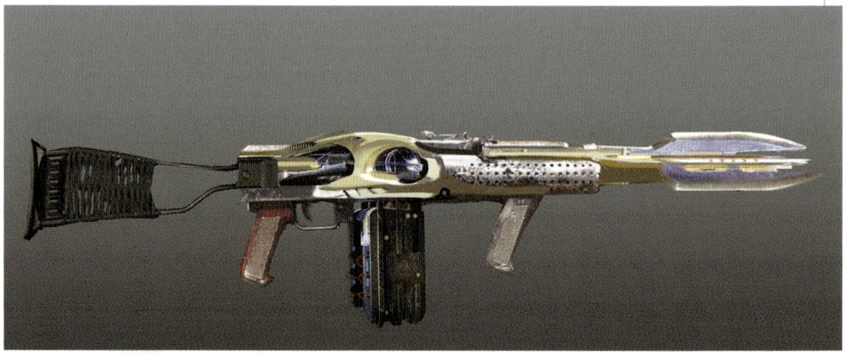

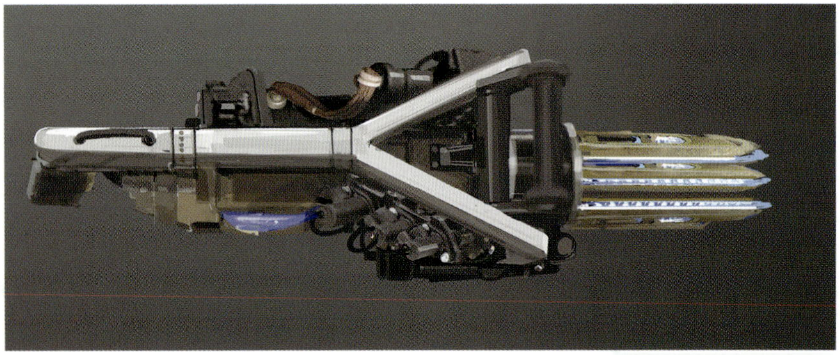

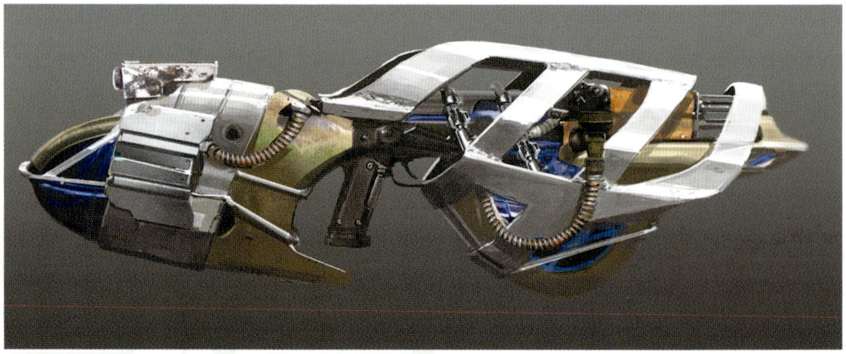

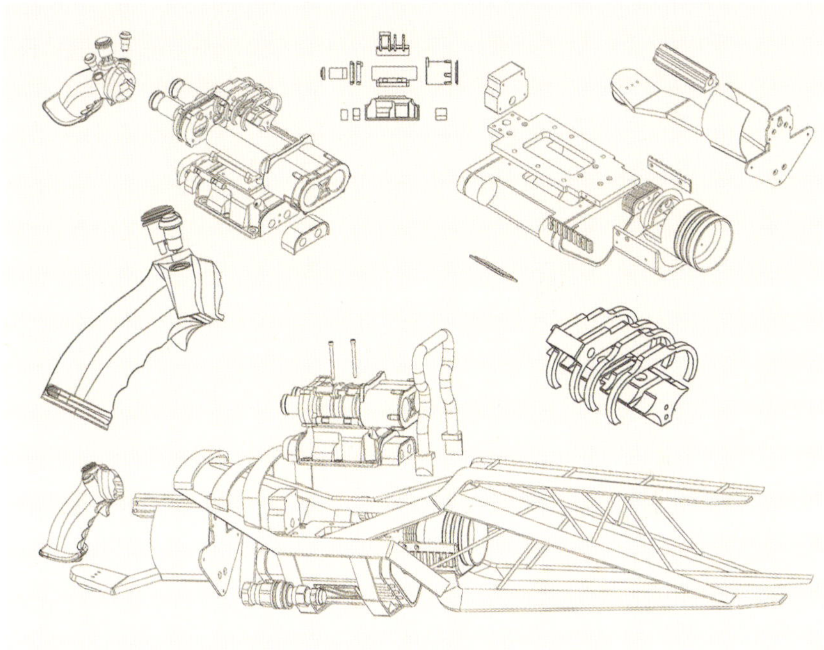

EAVES

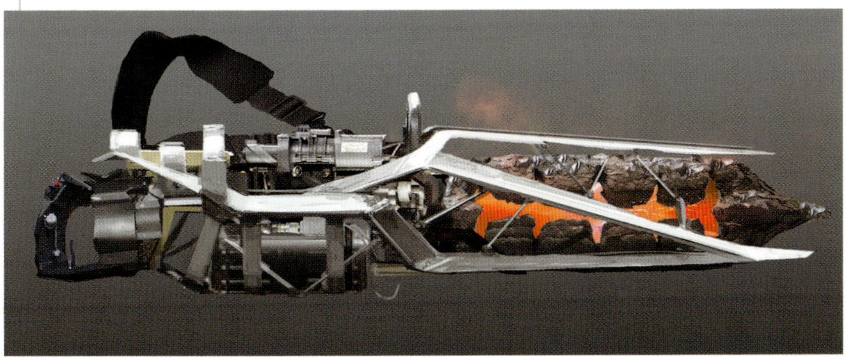

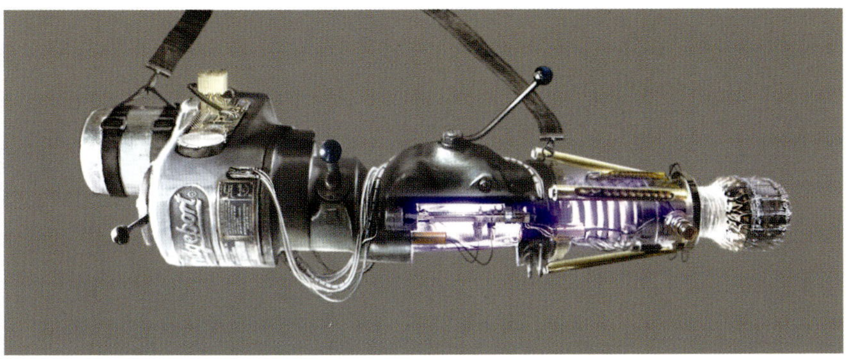

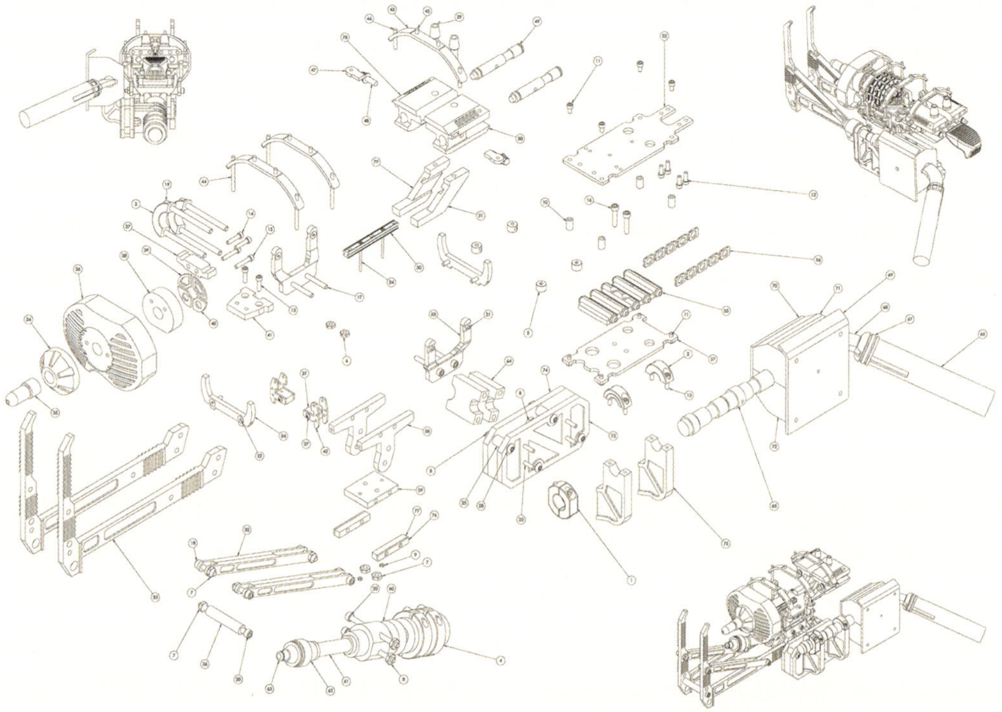

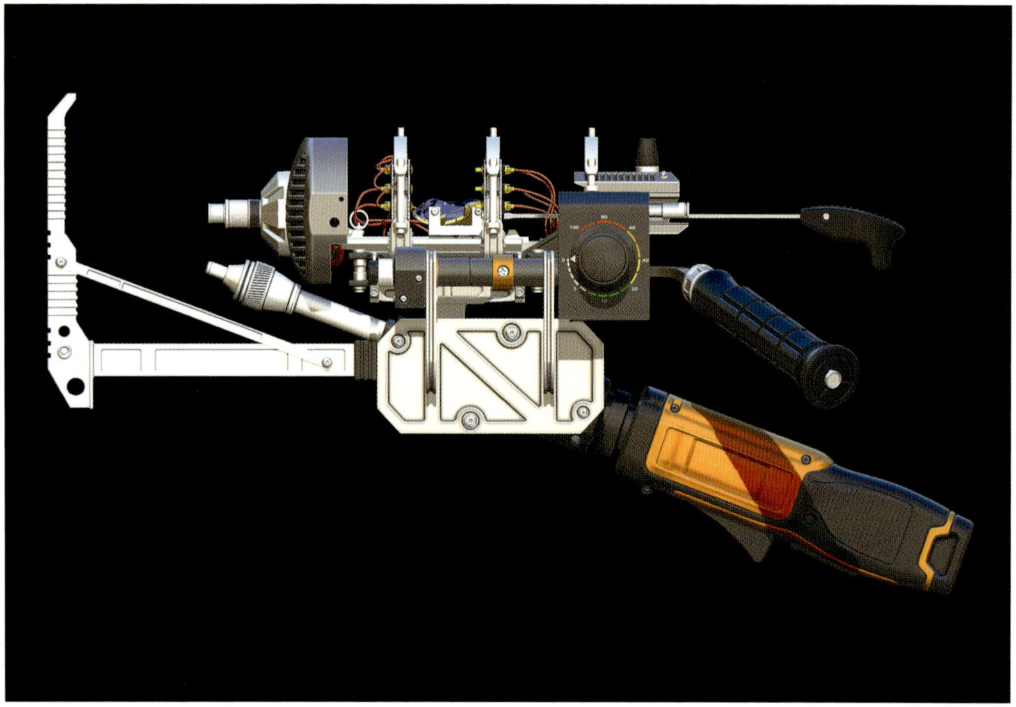

EAVES

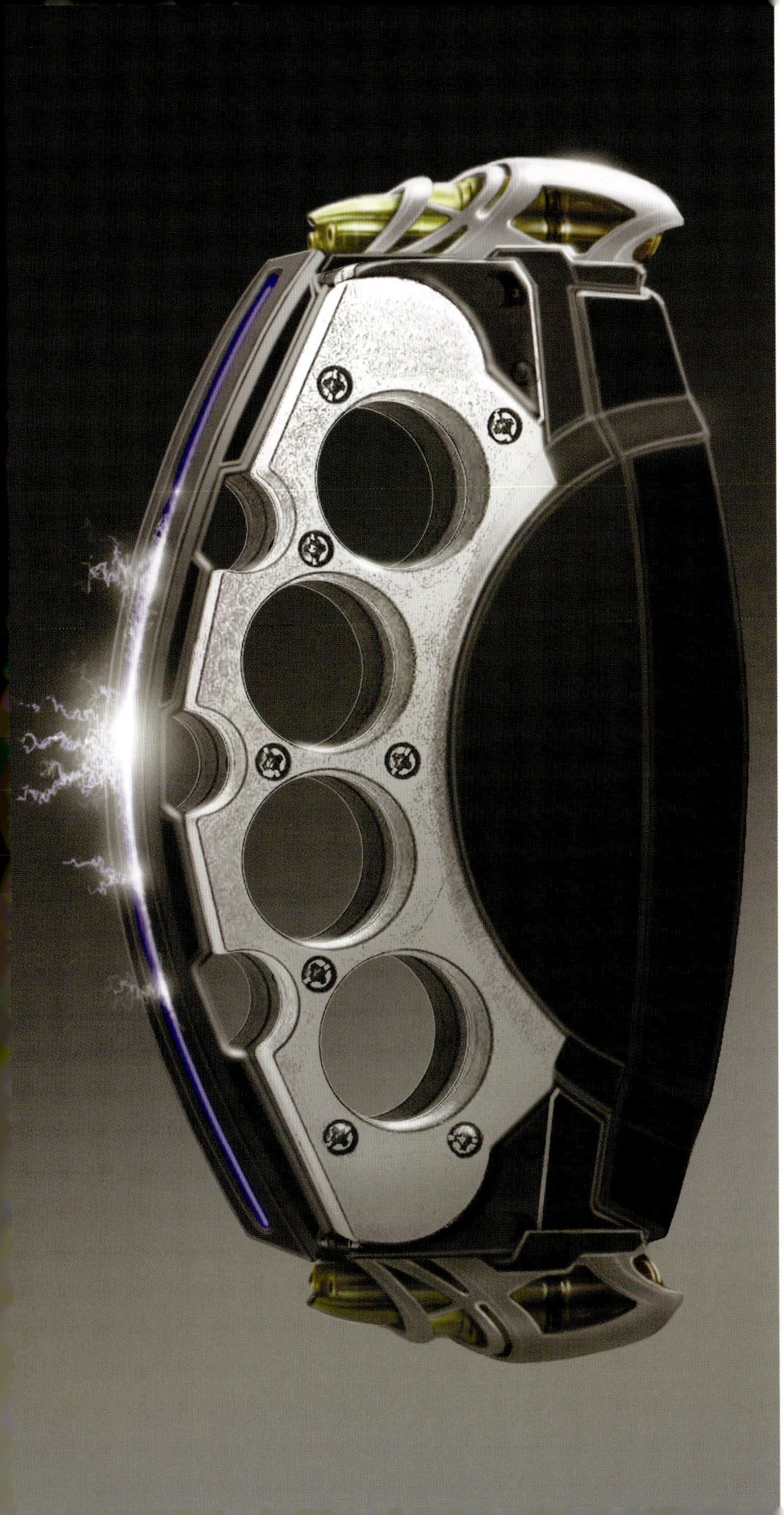

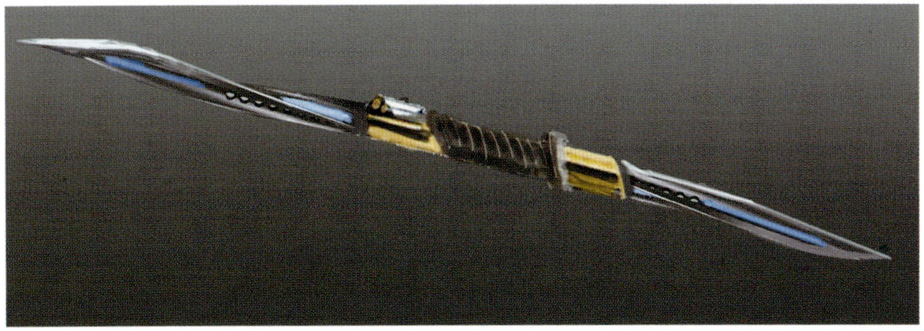

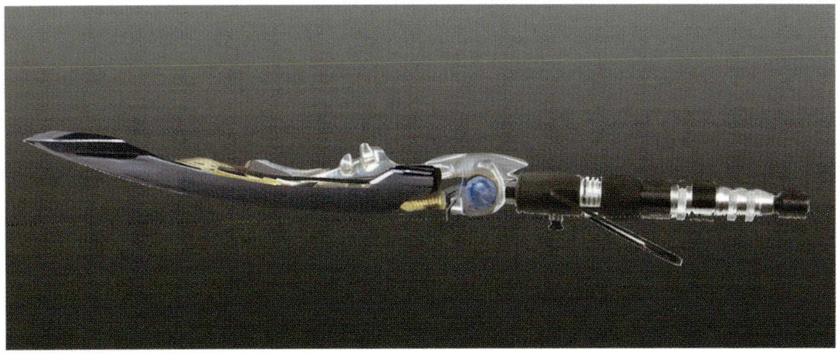

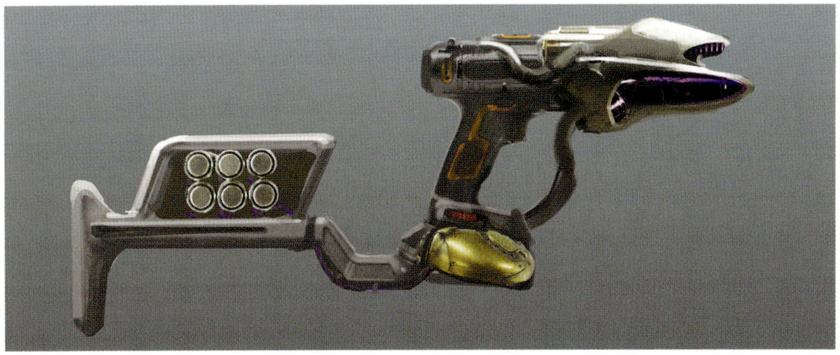

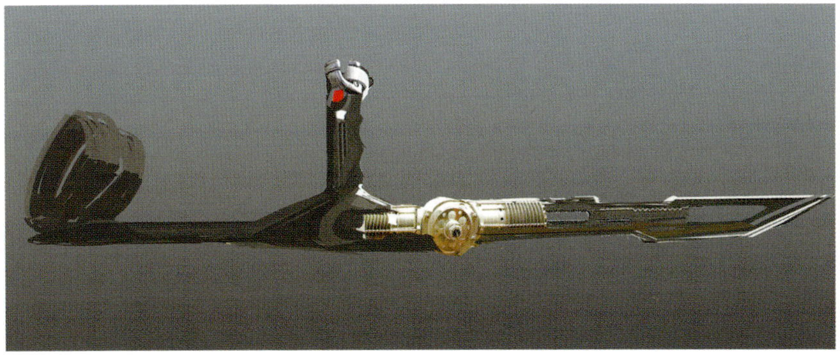

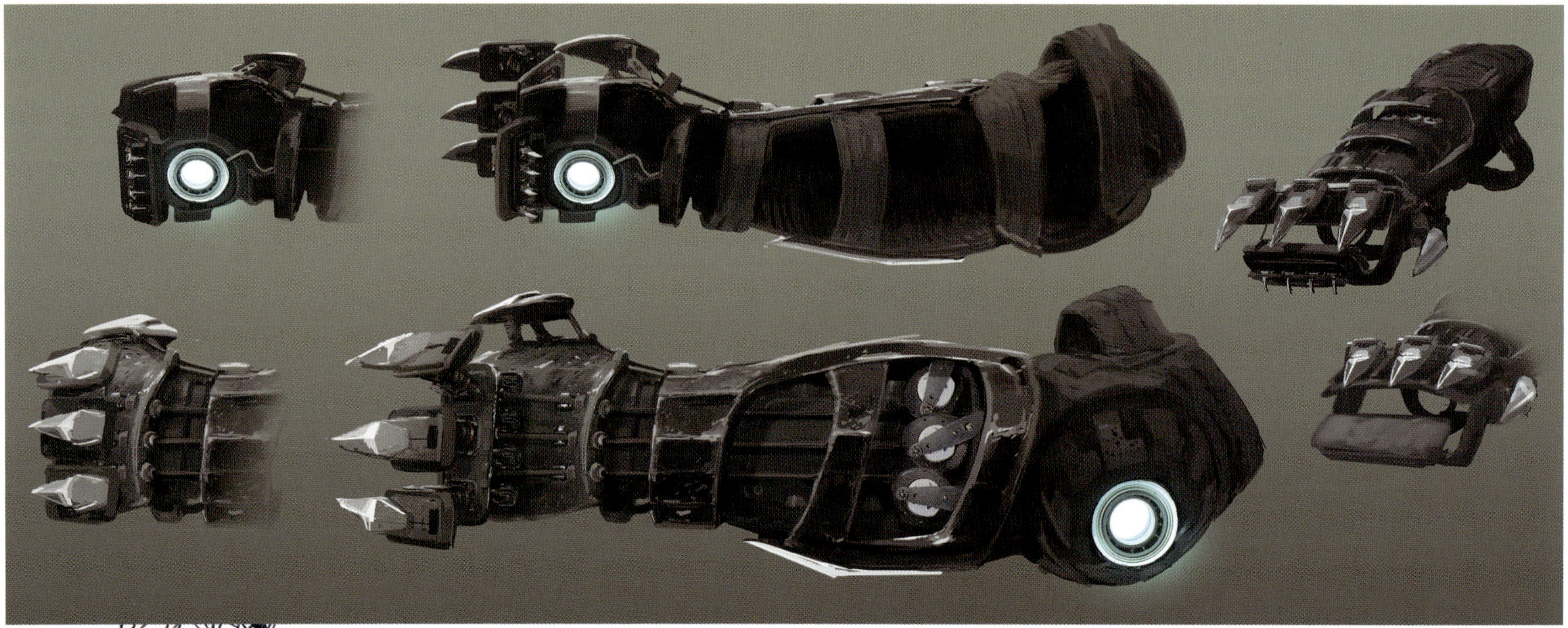

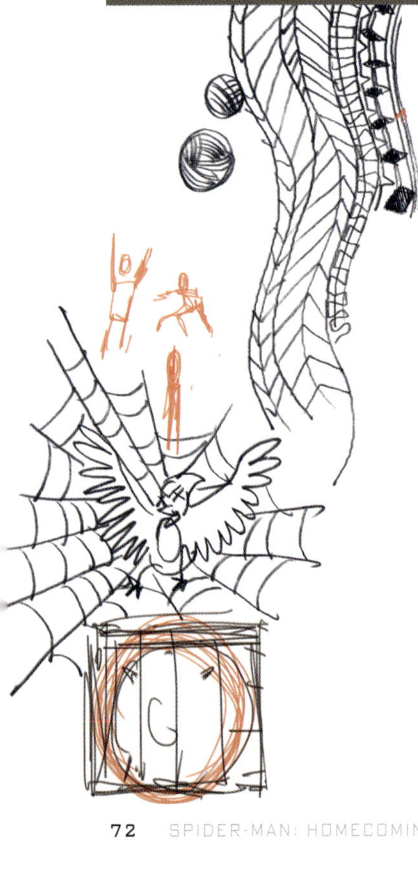

"What's great is that the hornet's nest that we're stirring up by Peter discovering this underground smuggling ring is just the tip of the iceberg of what may be bubbling below the surface, which I think allows us to go to some really amazing places and plant a lot of seeds of what could happen in the future of the series."
—Jon Watts

EAVES

Among several mashups of Chitauri and human technology seen throughout Toomes Salvage is the Ferry Cutter, used during a pivotal scene in the latter part of the film.

"We looked at chainsaws and concrete cutters, and we started to manipulate that with the Chitauri stuff. The concrete cutter had a really cool look. It was something that was portable that they could carry in with a handle, so it worked really well. For the cutter itself, in the beginning, the plan was to design two practical blades with the Chitauri stuff on it, and when it would spin, it would generate this laser cutter. But that didn't end up in the final version."
-John Eaves

EAVES

FUENTEBELLA

KUNITAKE

MASON

"Mason is a guy who's working for the Vulture. He's the guy that's tinkering on the stuff and making these crazy suits and putting this stuff together and packaging this stuff up so they can resell it to bad guys around the world."
— Jeremy Latcham

"Mason is always playing with something. Whether it is a piece of alien salvage or a reworked piece of Earth technology, all of the mini gadgets were there to show that his mind was always working on solving problems."
— Kirk Corwin

FUENTEBELLA

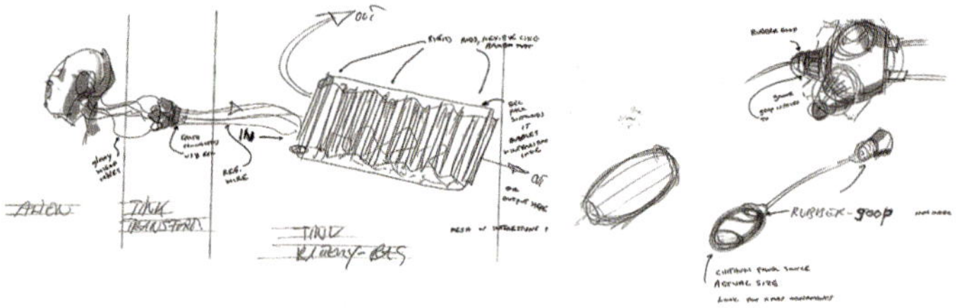

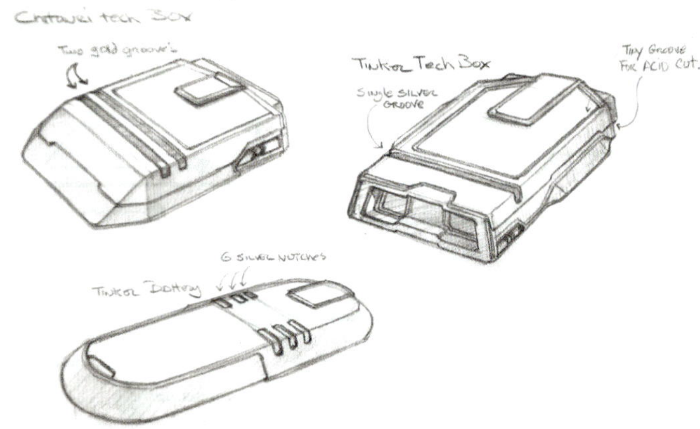
Chitauri tech Box
Two gold grooves
Tinker Tech Box
Single SILVER GROOVE
Tiny Groove For ACID Cut.
6 SILVER NOTCHES
Tinker Battery

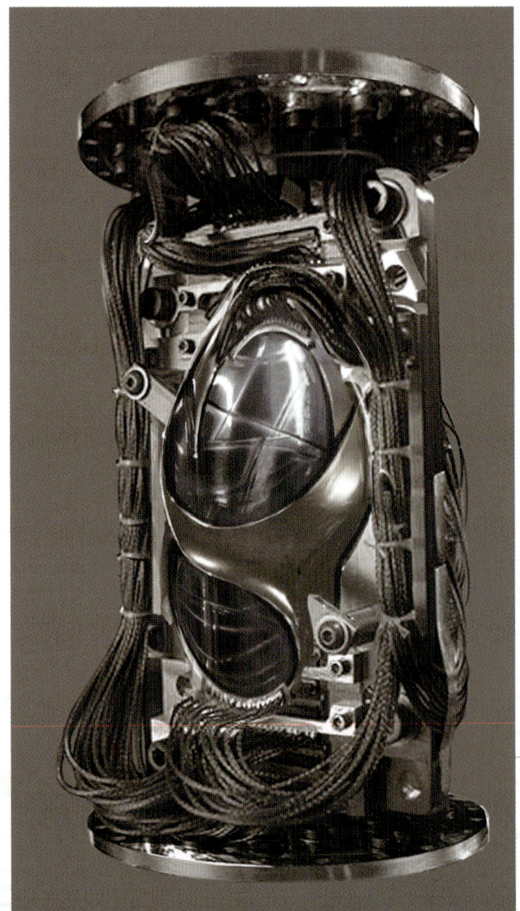

EAVES

NIZZI

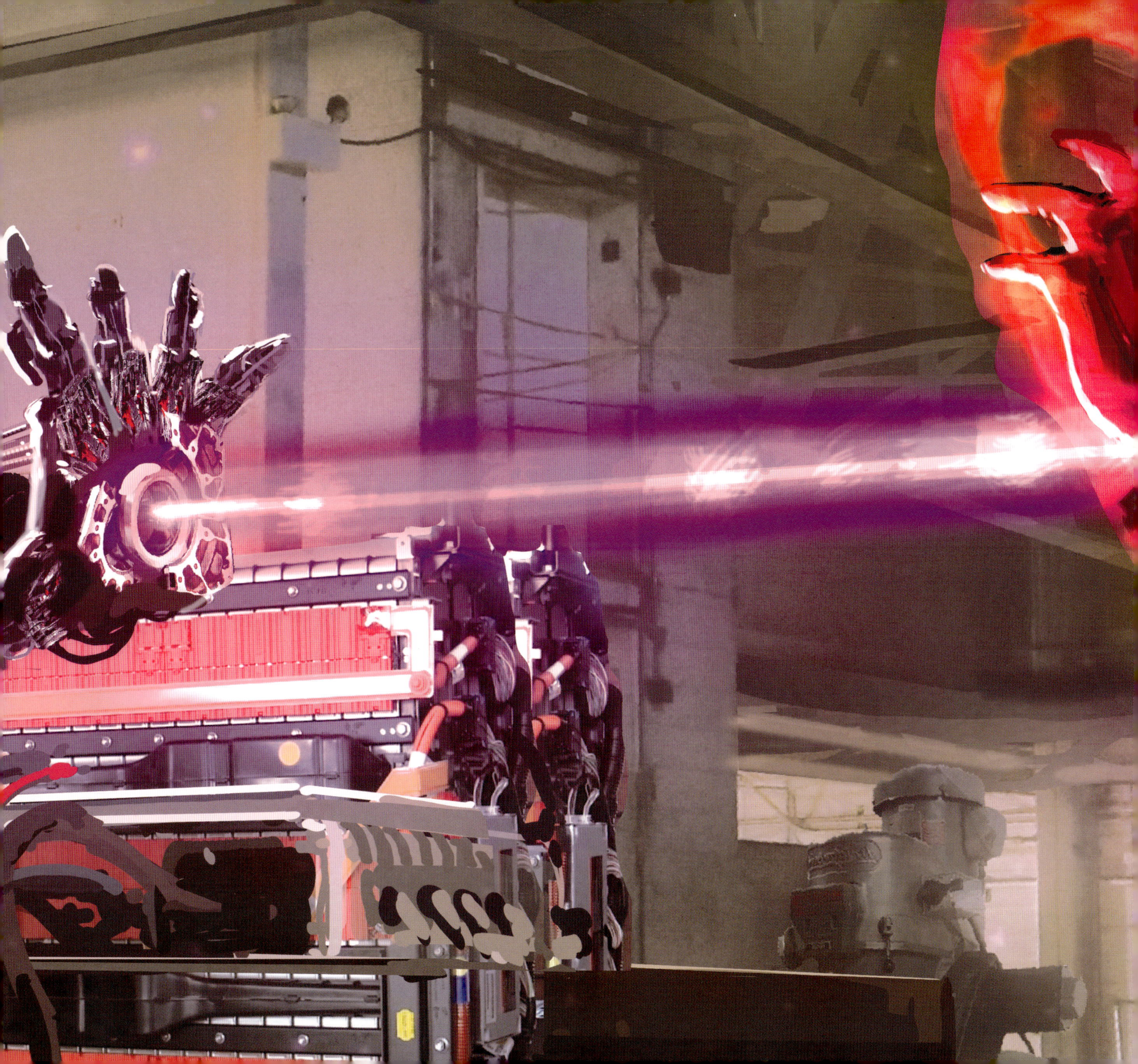

SHOCKER

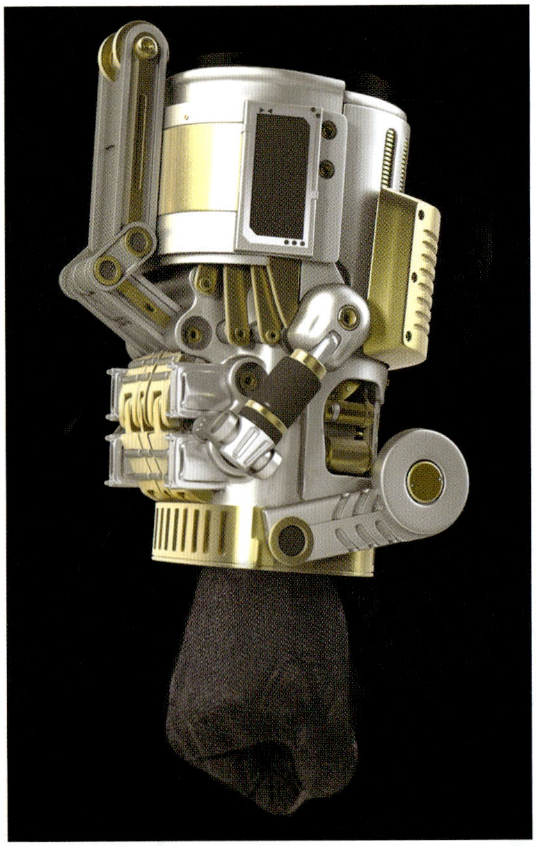

"For the Shocker, we wanted to not make it seem too much like a costumed character, but still be inspired by the original Shocker from the comics by giving him the same lines, coloring, and texture schemes. We also repurposed Crossbones' gauntlet from *Captain America: Civil War* into that Shocker look. Since a lot of the bad-guy tech comes from repurposed items that were stolen from other movies, we figured this could be another item that was altered."

— Concept Artist Rodney Fuentebella

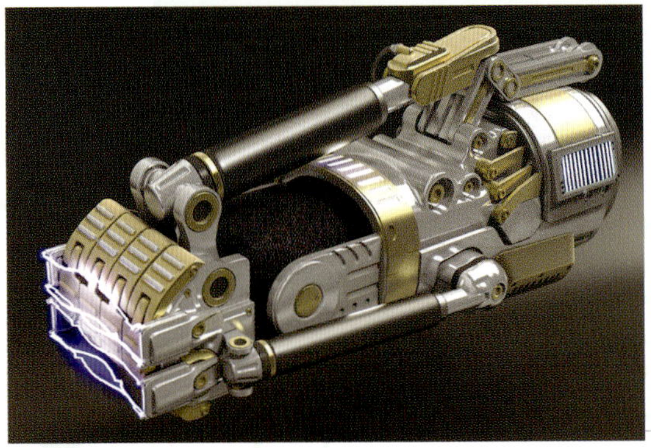

EAVES

PREVIOUS **KUNITAKE**

FUENTEBELLA

FUENTEBELLA

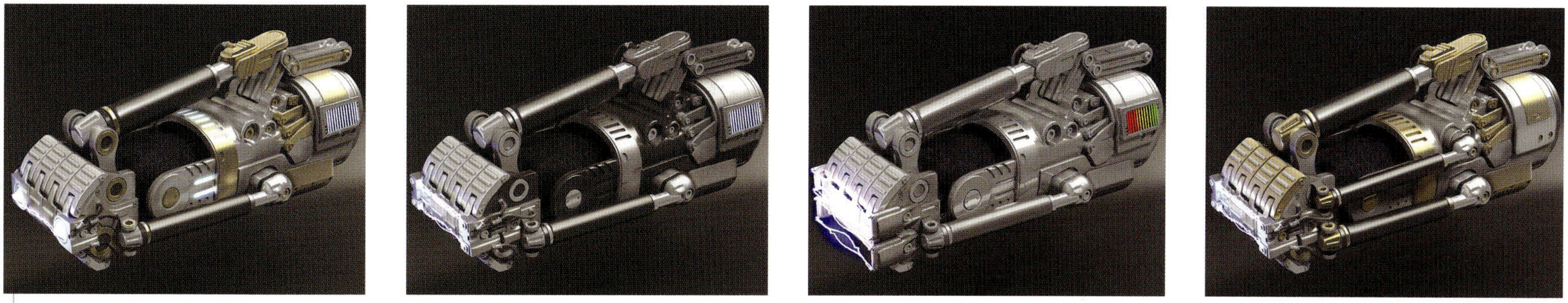

EAVES

FUENTEBELLA

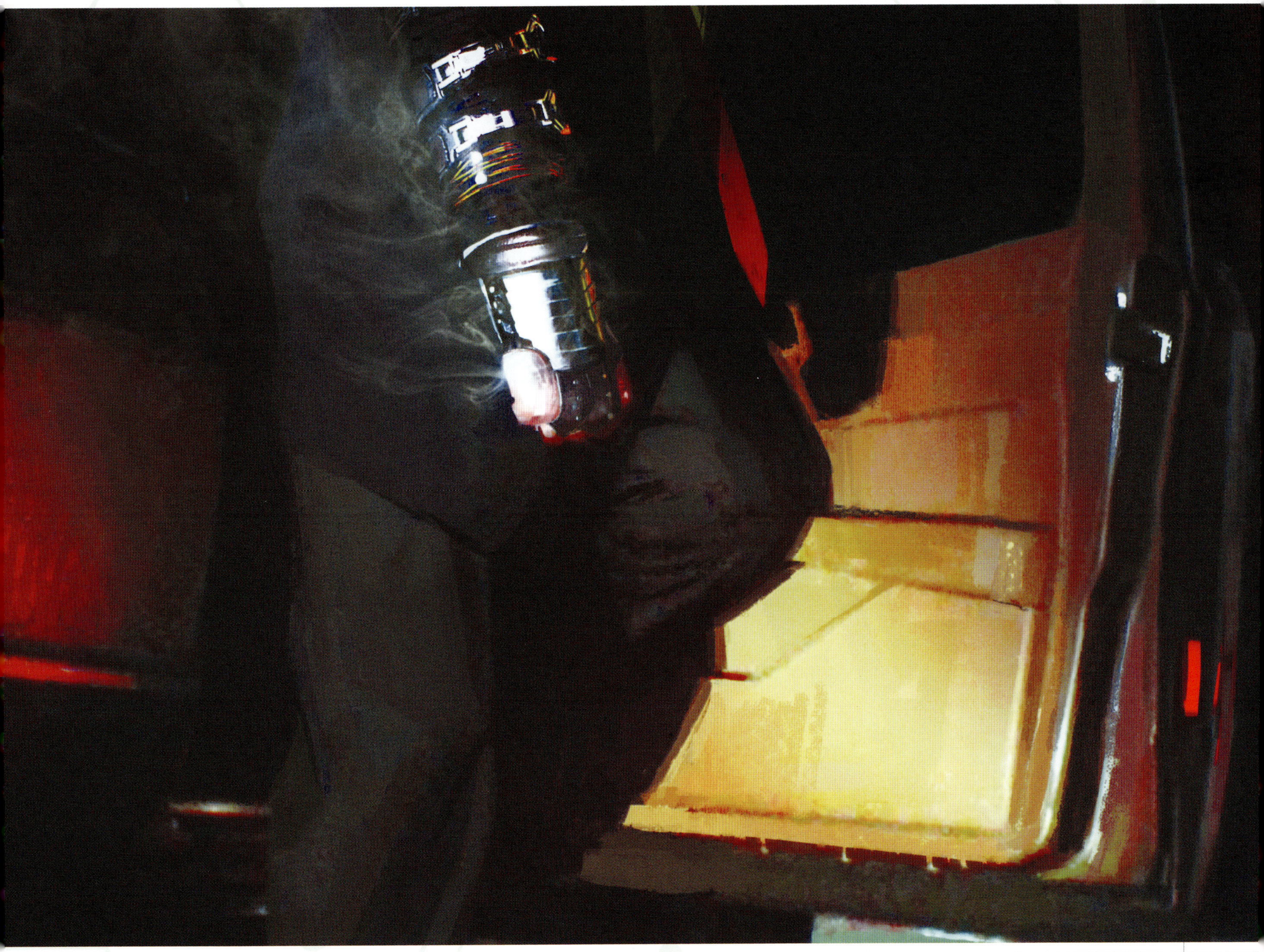

MANDRADJIEV

VULTURE

ADRIAN TOOMES

"The idea that you would just build a suit to look like a vulture is very showboaty, and somewhat old-fashioned. I think there's an element to that we can touch on, but for me it's more of why you would need a wing suit in the first place. And if you can come up with a good reason for him to need a wing suit, then it's just working backwards from there. Why is this real? Why would you have this? Why do you need to fly up to a certain height? If you fly up to a certain height, would you need a helmet? Do you need something for when there's no oxygen when you get to high altitude levels? Do you have to stay warm? Is this military technology? Or is it this a hacked sort of thing that the Tinkerer has built? How many personal embellishments would you put on this if it was basically custom made for you? So I think within that world, you get to have a lot of fun with why it looks the way it looks."

— **Jon Watts**

NIZZI

MANDRADJIEV | PREVIOUS MANDRADJIEV

NIZZI

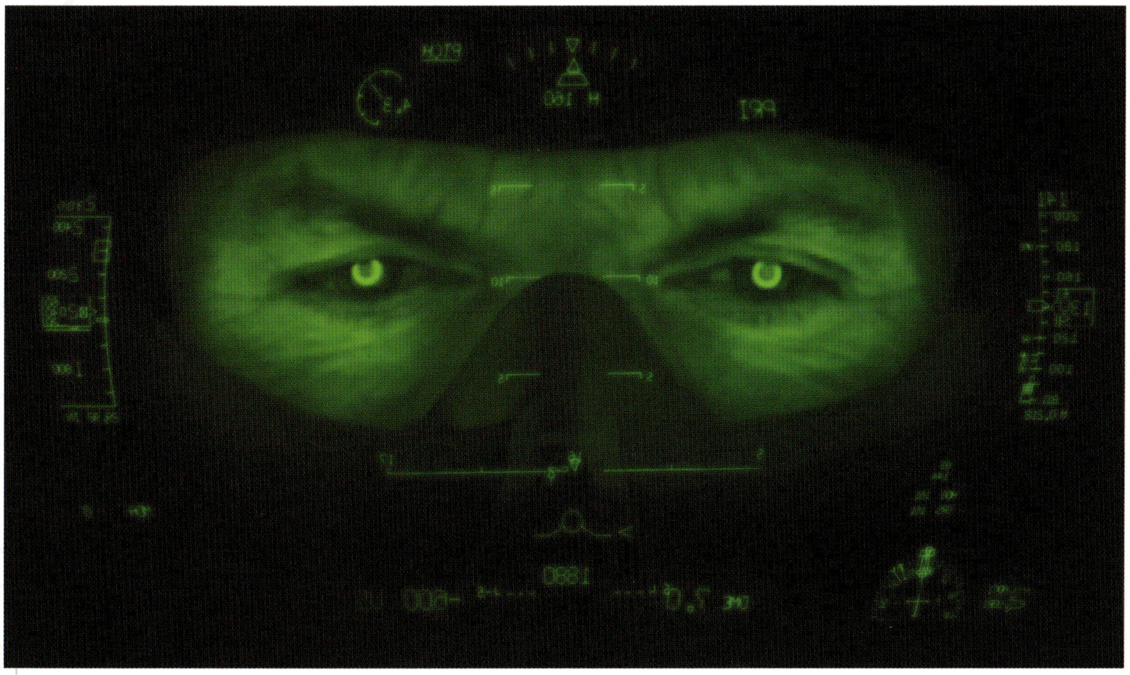

While most of the villains' tech was based on designs seen in previous MCU films, some of it was inspired by gear used by the U.S. military.

"The new F-35 Joint Strike Fighter helmets have this thing where there is eye-tracking on the face shield, and they have these green lights that project over the pilot's eyes—so it's kind of riffing off this technology. If he's flying at night, it can be kind of like night-vision goggles, and of course it can help convey the green color of the Vulture from the comics. It's a bit menacing. The outer green is also reflected inside the mask on the HUD display. It's also a little sinister in the way it highlights his face."
– Concept Artist Josh Nizzi

NIZZI

MEINERDING

NIZZI | MANDRADJIEV

MEINERDING

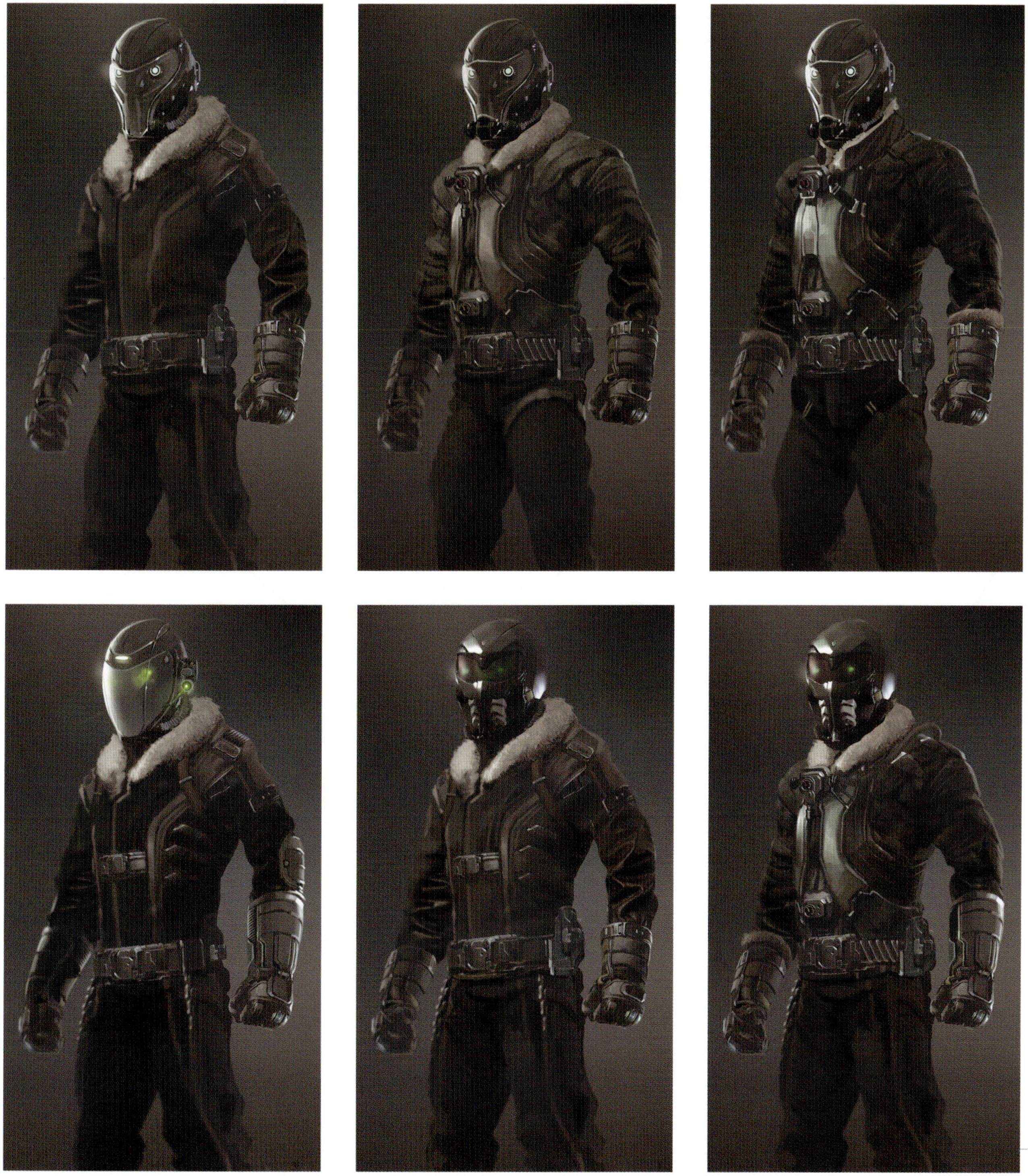

"The first fabric we looked at for the Vulture ended up being too shiny. The final trousers were made from actual 'new' old stock World War II fabric. It was beautifully colored and proportioned, and looked absolutely perfect for the character. Sometimes wonderful fabric does exist, it's just hard to get ahold of."
— Costume Designer Louise Frogley

FUENTEBELLA

NIZZI

MEINERDING

FUENTEBELLA

MANDRADJIEV

NIZZI

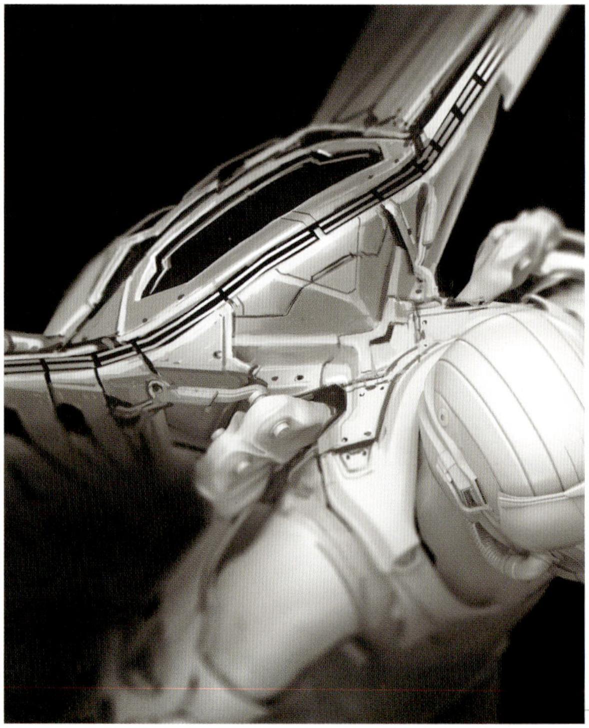

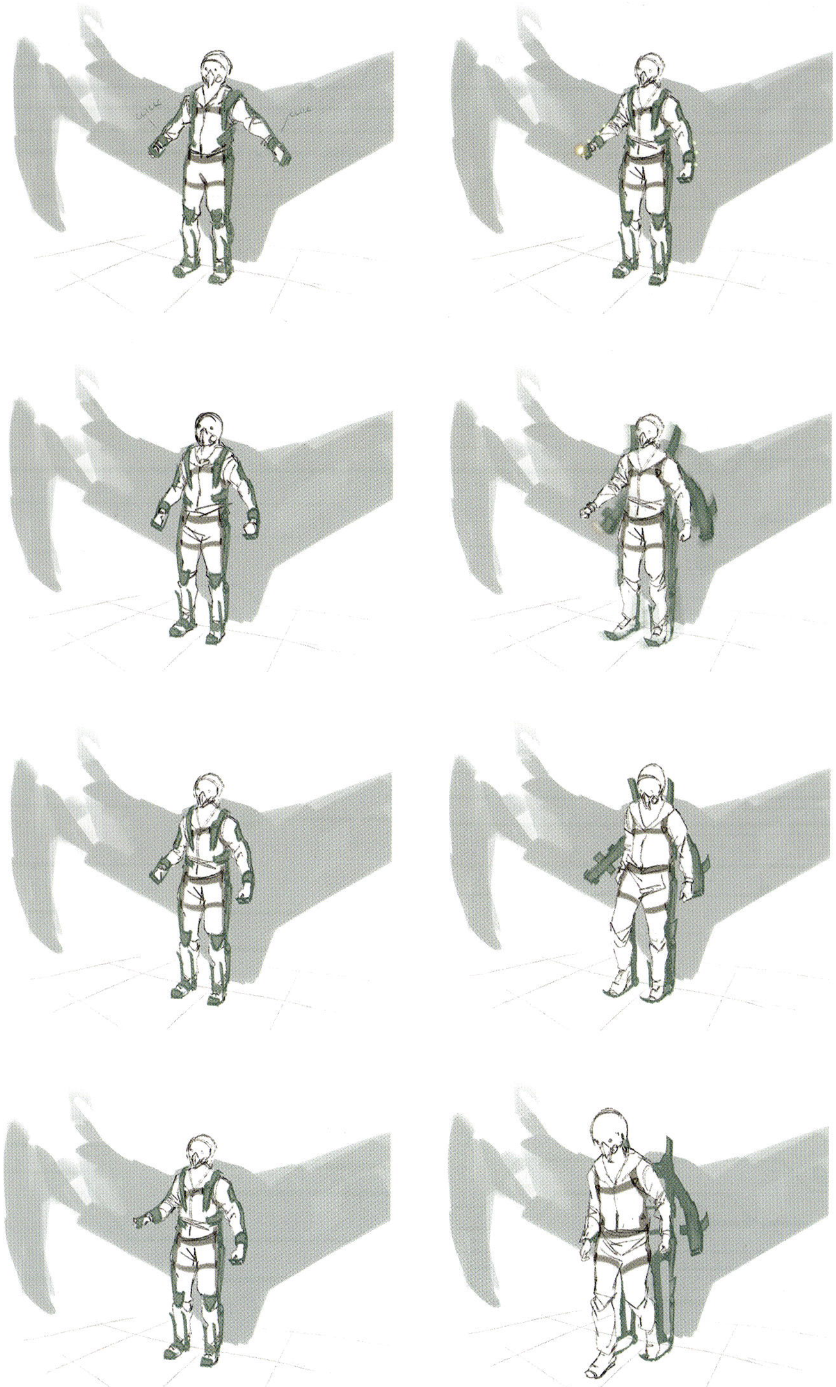

The Vulture suit is a massive piece of machinery. Once the concept started to take shape, other factors had to be considered in the overall design—such as how someone would get in and out of the suit.

"I made several sketches of the Vulture just going in and out of the suit. I wanted it to use the same mechanics as a roller coaster, that way of being strapped on, and I wanted it to feel like it fit in with the overall mechanics of the design."
– Rodney Fuentebella

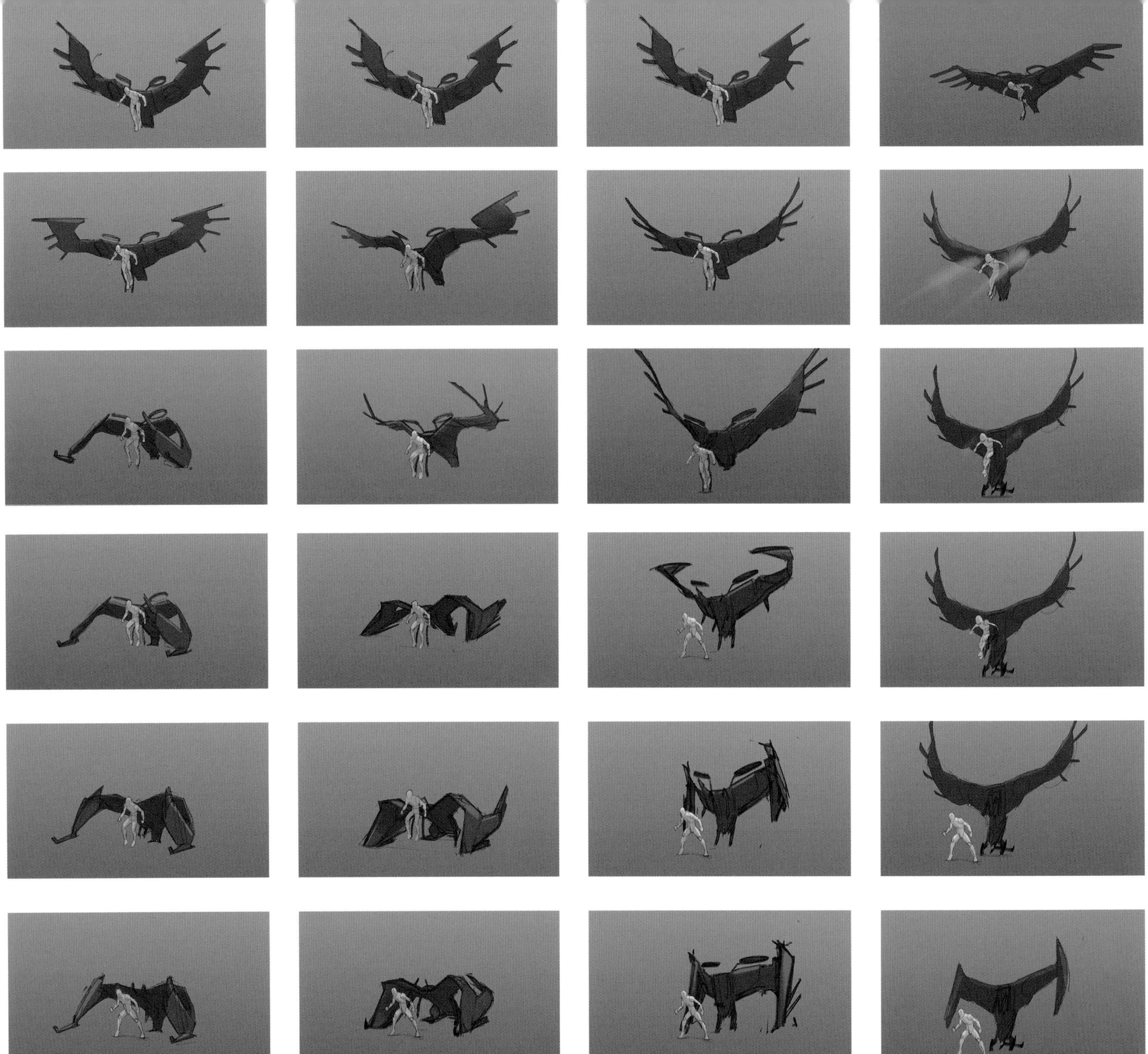

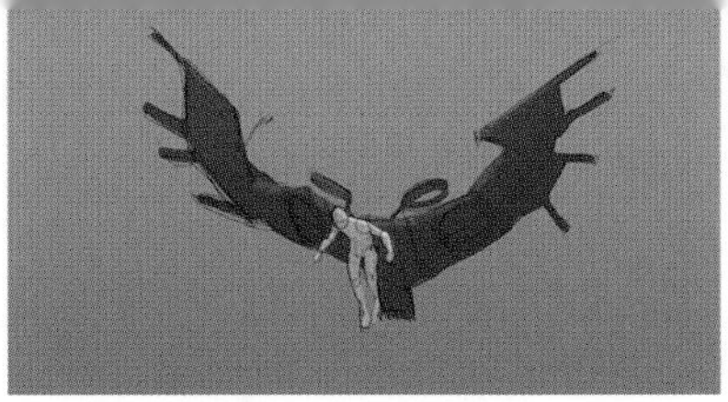
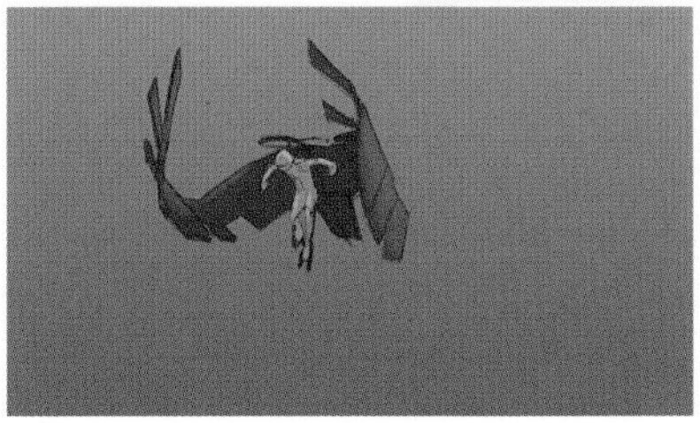

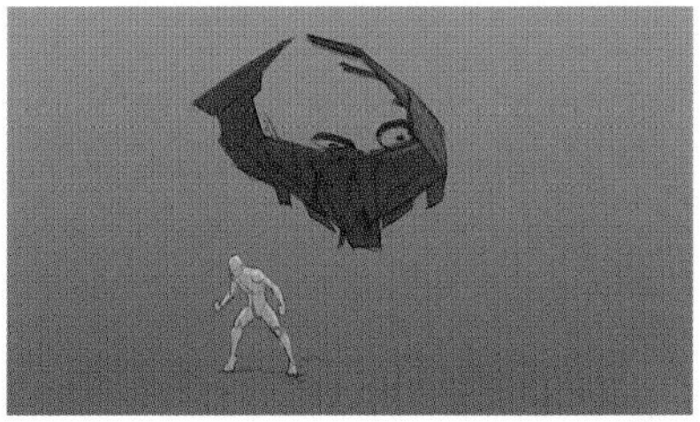

NIZZI

"The idea was to make it less like the Falcon's backpack wings and more like a vehicle. So the wings got larger and the suit got bigger, and it really kind of set it apart from the Falcon stuff. I think a lot of it was trying to find the balance in the design, and trying to find poses that could work with the mass. The wings had to have enough articulation in them so that they could get into these poses where he could fight Spider-Man one-on-one, and not always be flying around in the air like an airplane. And because of how it's articulated, you can still kind of get that Vulture shape and then allow the wings to fold up or hang down."

– Josh Nizzi

FUENTEBELLA

NIZZI

OZZIMO

HERMAN

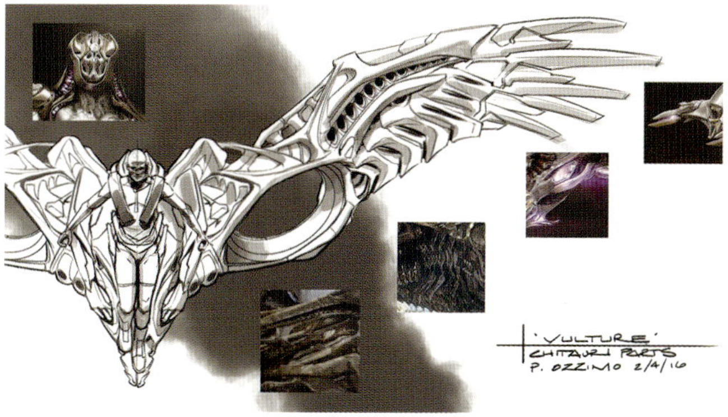

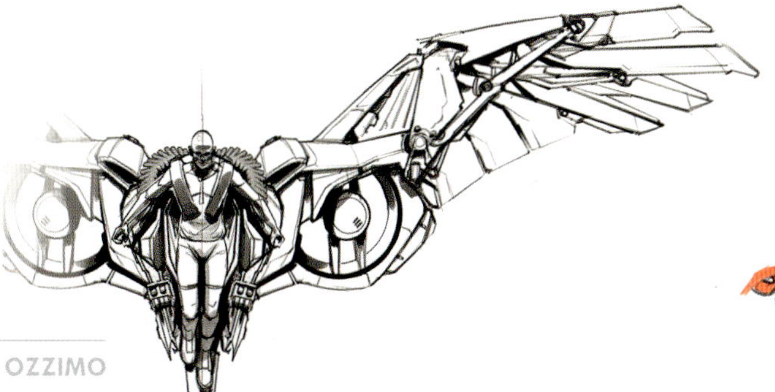

OZZIMO

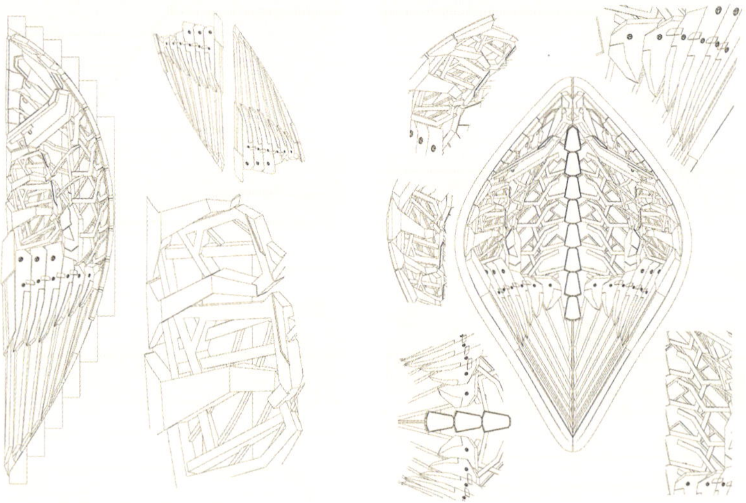

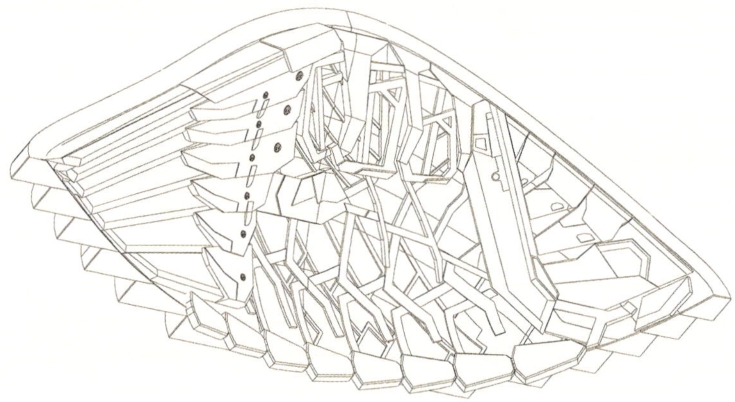

"The suit needed to be able to attach itself to an airplane to form an airtight, pressurized cocoon. It was just a process of taking the Vulture model and finding a way to wrap the wings. The African black egret is able to wrap its wings around itself and create a shadow to see through the water. The bird helped give us a structure for how to create that kind of dome shape."
– Concept Artist Phil Saunders

OZZIMO

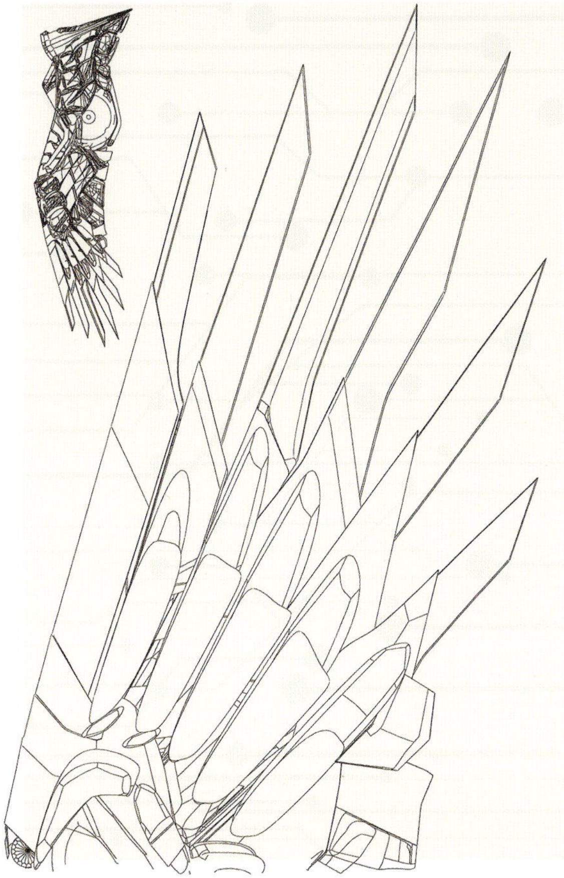

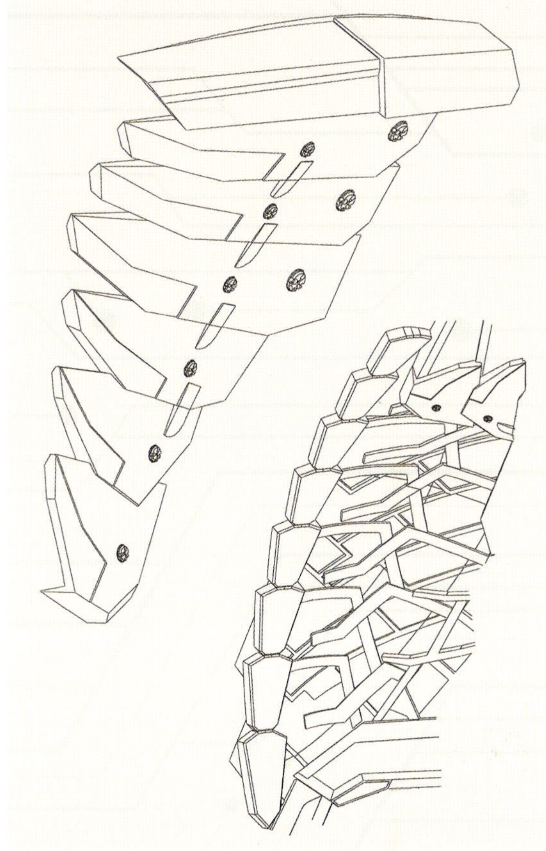

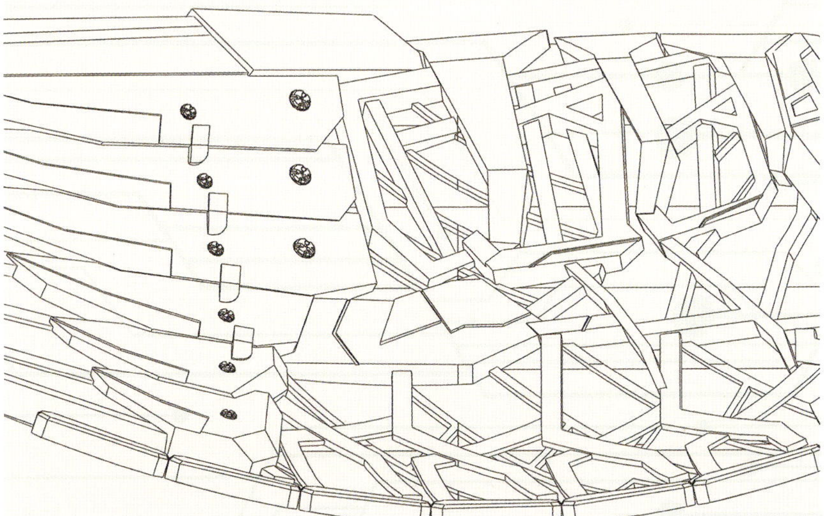

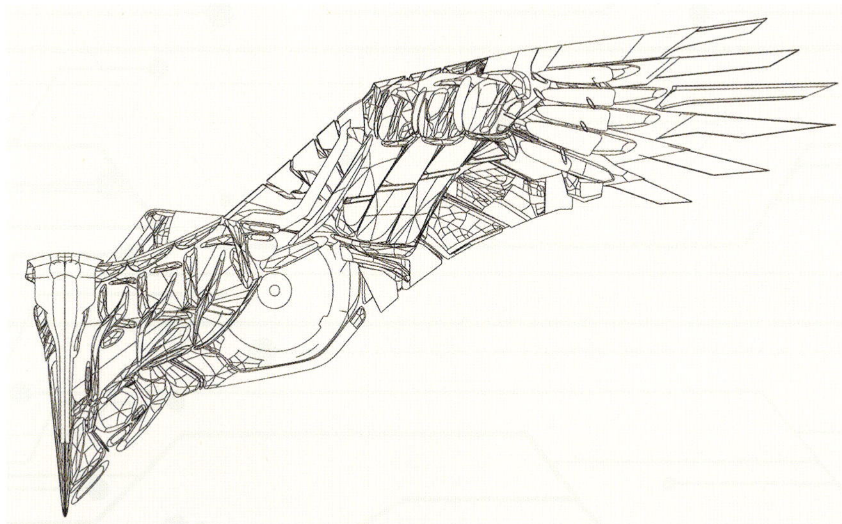

SAUNDERS

NIZZI

NIZZI

MEINERDING

NIZZI

OZZIMO

SAUNDERS

NIZZI

FUENTEBELLA

MEINERDING

"Initially, the Vulture was going to be somebody with previous ties to the Falcon, so we purposely tied him visually to that a little bit, with an ex-military look. The wings and gear were always supposed to look a bit cobbled-together, kind of like a prototype version—a larger, clunkier version of what the Falcon has."
– Josh Nizzi

NIZZI

| OZZIMO

FOURTH PERIOD

AFTER-SCHOOL ACTIVITIES

GO OUT AND GET MOVING! Midtown has always encouraged students to pursue interests outside the classroom. Spend time with friends in a club after the bell rings. Apply for an internship, or volunteer to help clean up our city streets. By being part of our local community, we'll all be better prepared to deal with whatever life throws our way!

> “[Peter] lives in an apartment with his aunt, and needs to go to school and needs to do his homework and needs to have an excuse for why he was out 15 minutes past his curfew. So when you're doing that and you have to stop the robbery down the street or uncover this bad guy that is beginning to do things within the neighborhood, it becomes very difficult. And that becomes his great struggle.
>
> **— Producer and Marvel Studios President Kevin Feige**”

MEINERDING

PREVIOUS **NIZZI**

Learning to juggle responsibilities is never easy—but for a teenager with crimefighting on his to-do list, high school has never felt so hard. Even for a smart kid like Peter Parker, finding the time to do it all can seem downright impossible—but that doesn't mean he's not trying.

"What's so great about Spider-Man when Steve Ditko and Stan Lee brought him to life in the early '60s is that he was such a great contrast to all the other Marvel heroes. He wasn't a wealthy industrialist billionaire. He wasn't a Norse god from Asgard. He wasn't a scientist who'd had an experiment go wrong and turned into an Incredible Hulk. He wasn't a Super-Soldier from the 1940s. He was a modern-day high-school kid in New York City who ended up accidentally getting extraordinary abilities. And what was so fun was to see a kid who had all the problems that we all have, that had all of the flaws that we have, that had all of the struggles we have. I have to do my homework. I have to get home on time. Is the girl going to go out with me to the dance? Am I going to just be somebody that has no social life? What—who am I?"
— Kevin Feige

MEINERDING

TAMM

MEINERDING

QUEEN'S BANK

S BANK

MEINERDING | PREVIOUS MEINERDING

PUI

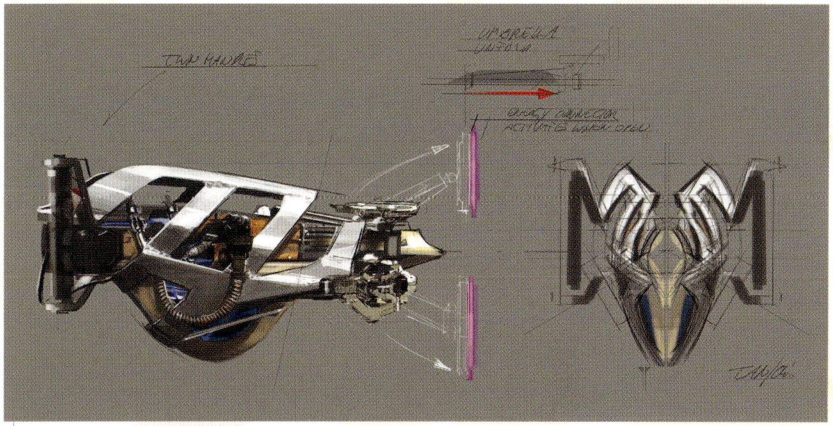

SCHOLL

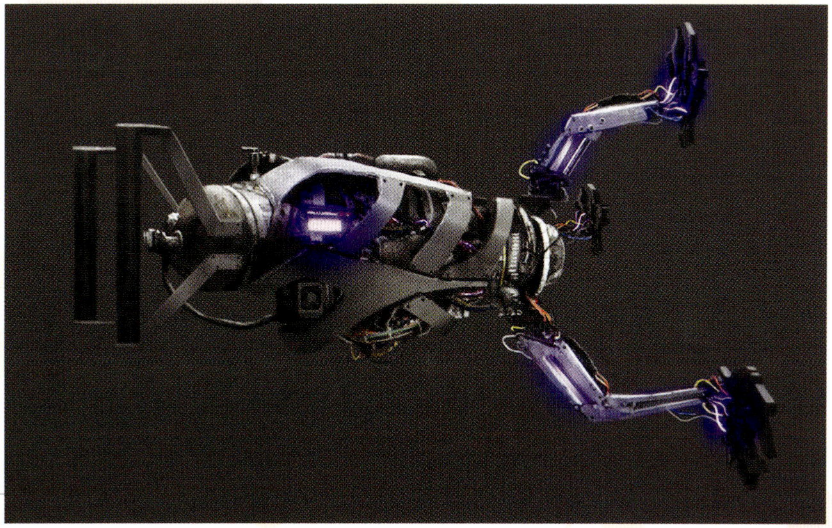

EAVES

TAMM

"Imagine if you were Spider-Man. Imagine if you had Spider-Man's abilities and could do all this amazing stuff. You would spend every moment of your day trying to maximize the amount of time you get to be Spider-Man, because it would be the best feeling in the world."
— Director Jon Watts

While attending a party thrown by classmate Liz Allan, Peter notices a bright glow in the distance. Investigating, he inadvertently stumbles upon a criminal enterprise specializing in the dealing and distribution of manipulated alien technology.

"These guys are selling things that they shouldn't be selling and are doing things they shouldn't be doing and threatening people they shouldn't be threatening. And power corrupts. The more powerful they become, the worse they become. And of course, Spider-Man's going to step in and put a stop to it. The fun part is Spider-Man's the only person who could even notice it's happening, right? Because Tony Stark's living at the top of Avengers Tower. The Avengers are running around the world, flying around in Quinjets, doing all these impressive things—but they're not with these people on the ground. Peter Parker's on the ground living with this stuff."
— Executive Producer Jeremy Latcham

TAMM

MEINERDING

MEINERDING

MANDRADJIEV

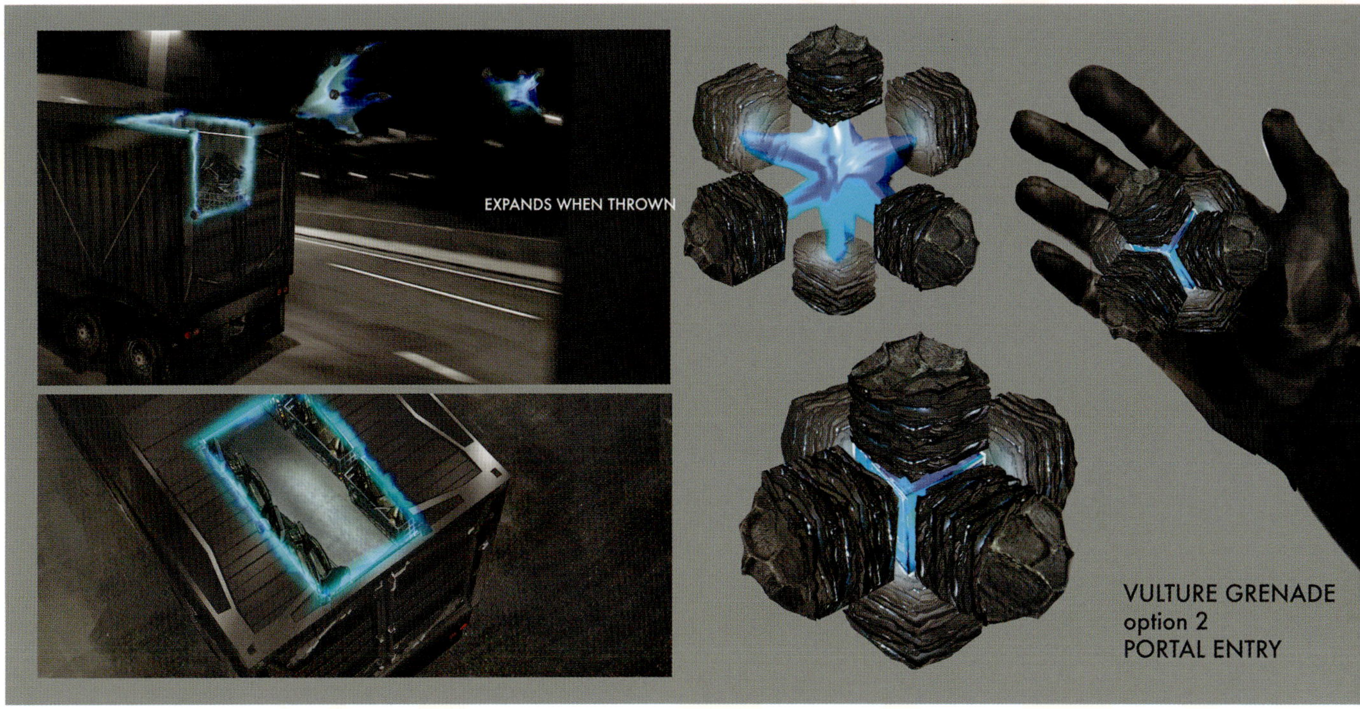
EXPANDS WHEN THROWN
VULTURE GRENADE
option 2
PORTAL ENTRY

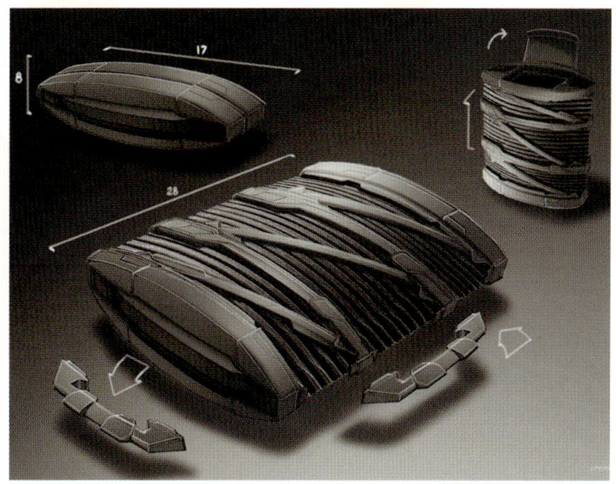
17
8
28

EAVES

TAMM

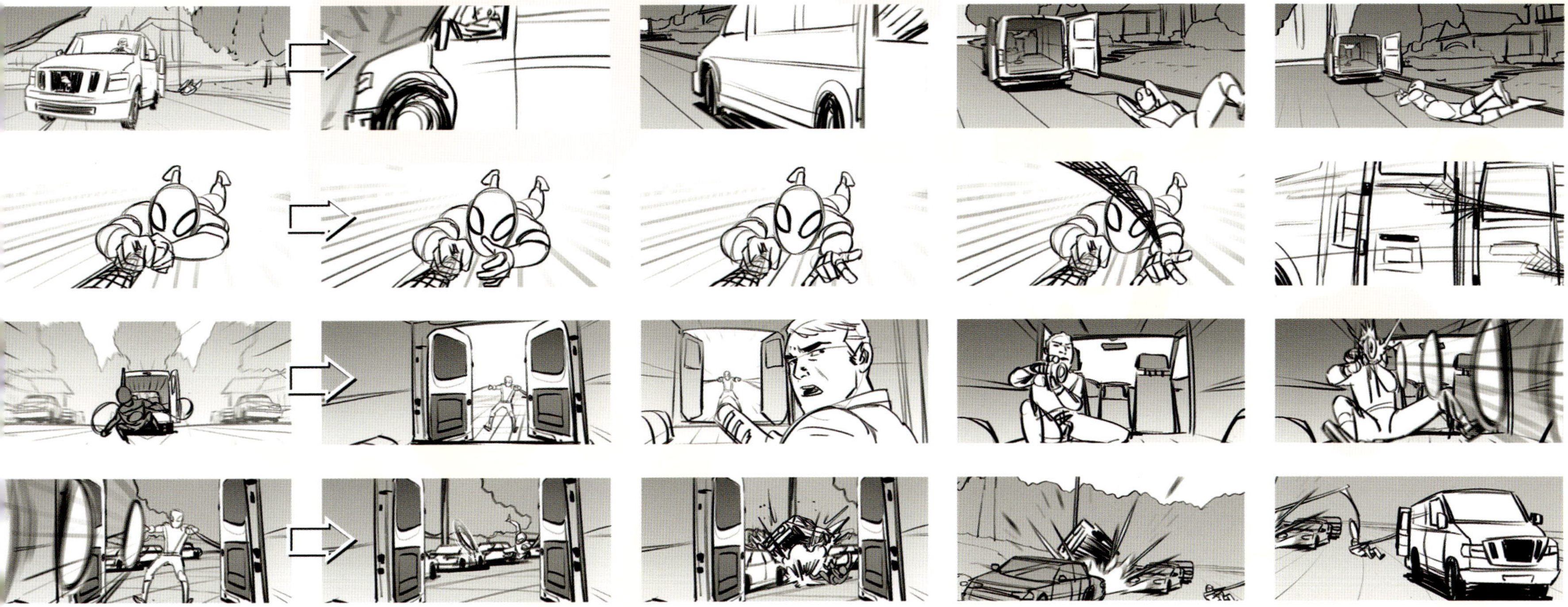

MANDRADJIEV | PREVIOUS MANDRADJIEV

LANGONE

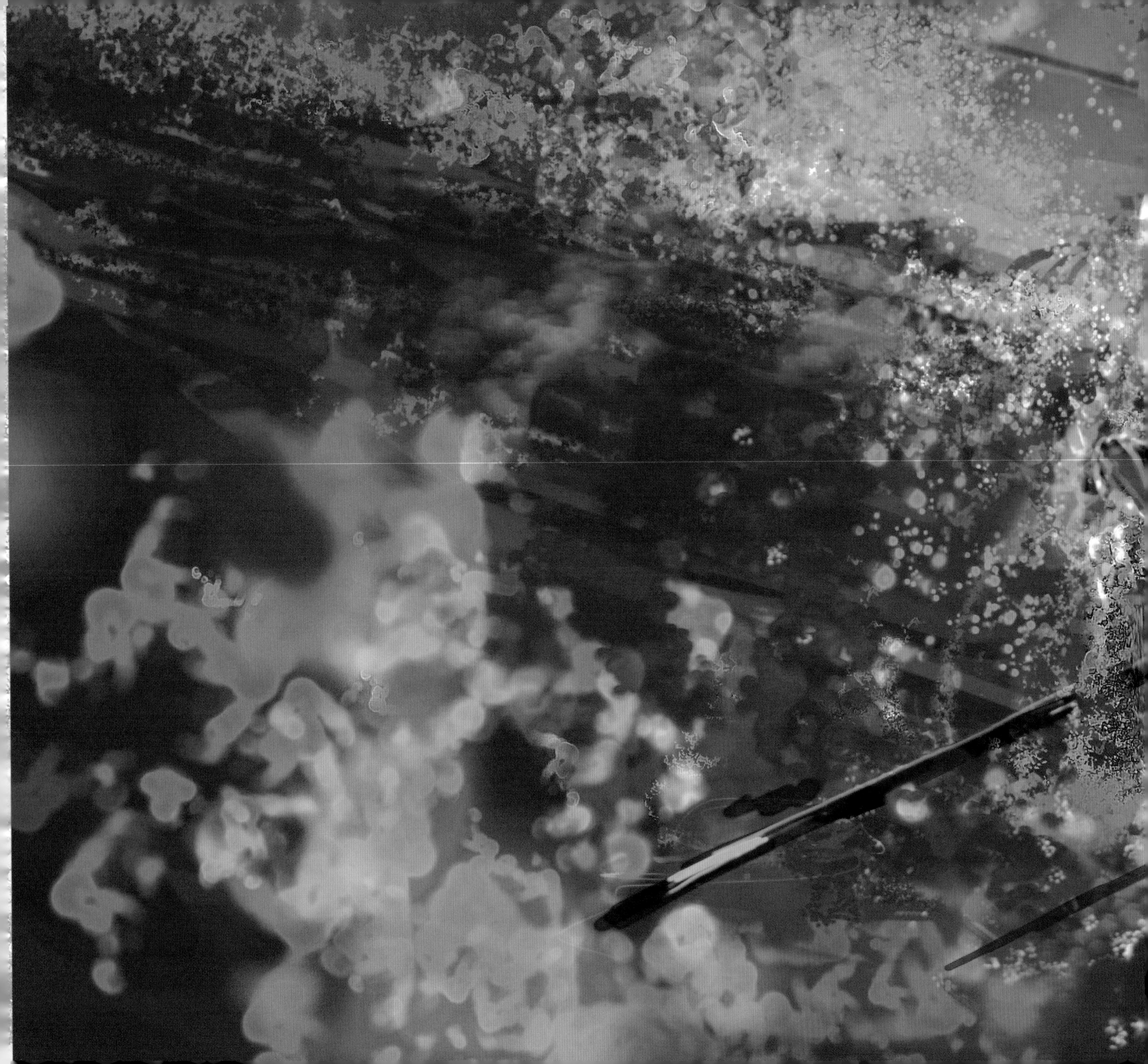

STARK INDUSTRIES

SCIENCE & TECHNOLOGIES INTERNSHIP

What will future Midtown graduates become? Will Flash Thompson be president? Perhaps Liz Allan will find a cure for cancer. Sophomore Peter Parker is on track to becoming a leader in the tech industry, thanks to his internship at Stark Industries. Peter is the lucky recipient of a grant enabling him to learn from the great tech guru and innovator himself, Tony Stark—when he's not busy being Iron Man, of course! We are so honored that one of our own was chosen from what we can only assume was a pool ofthousands of applicants for such a prestigious position!
CONGRATULATIONS, PETER!

MEINDERING

SAUNDERS

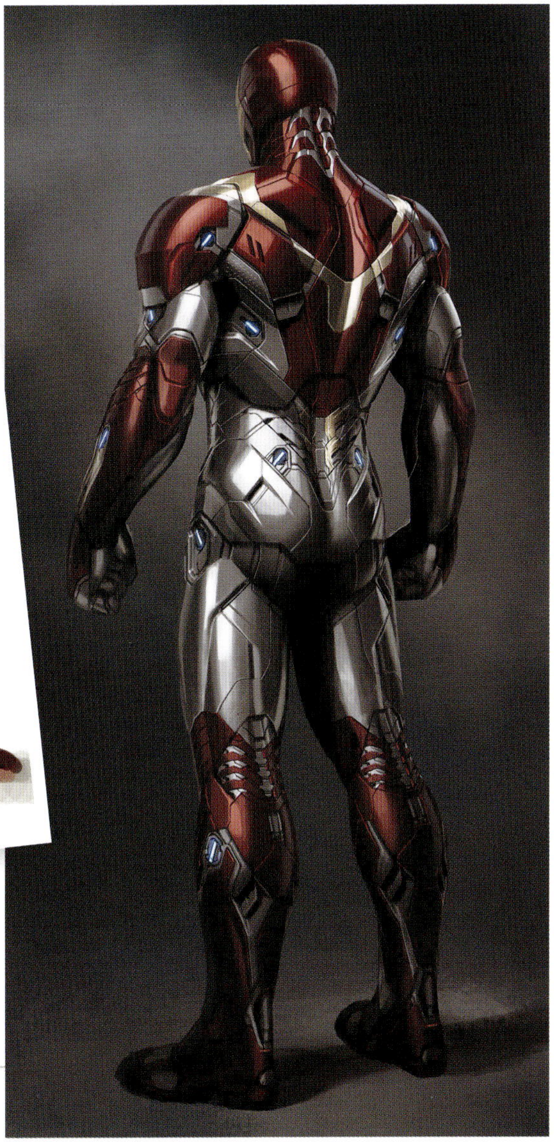

140–141, 148–155 **MEINERDING,**
144–145 **FUENTEBELLA**
142–143, 146–147 **MANDRADJIEV**

SAUNDERS

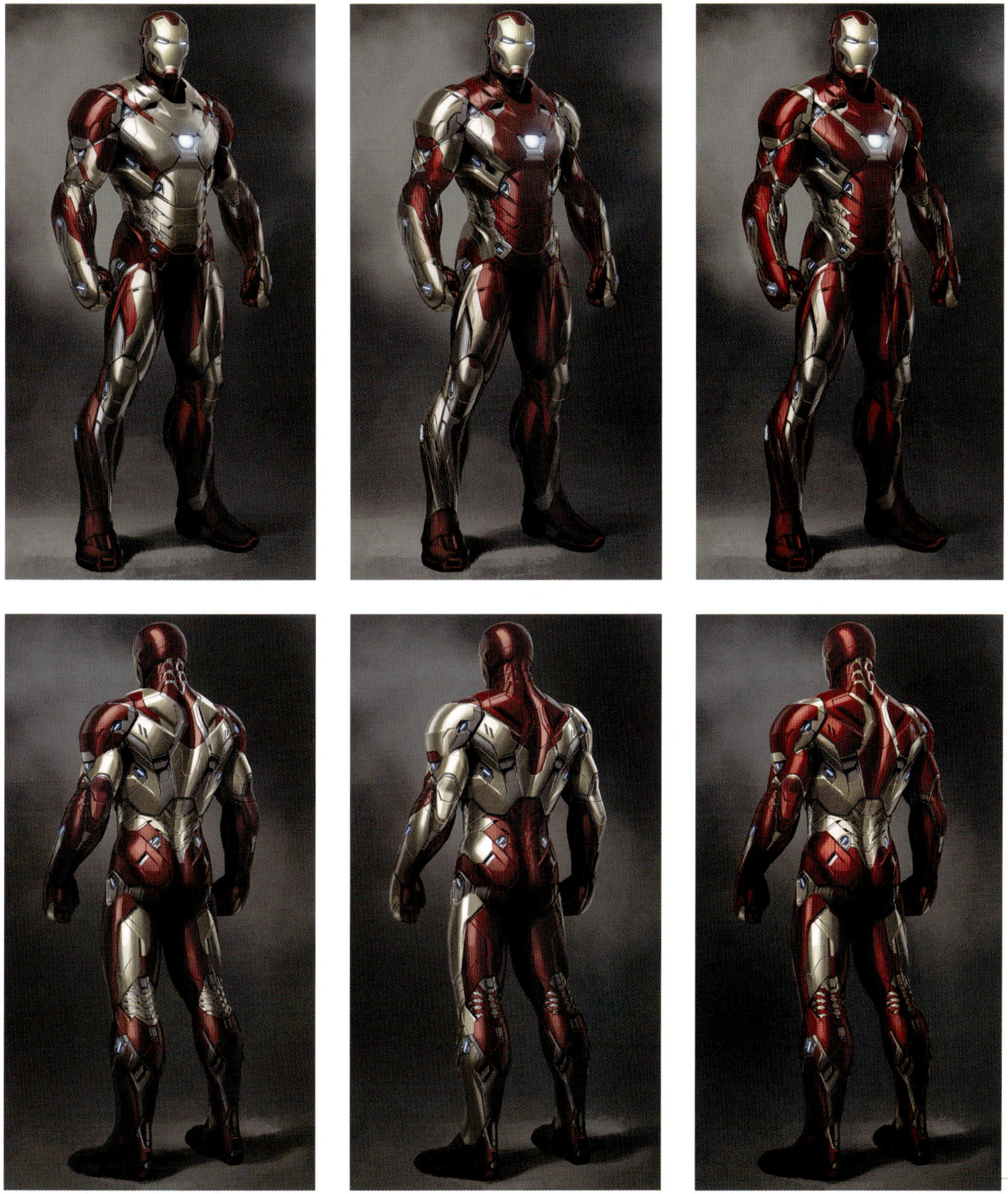

Iron Man hasn't changed much since his last appearance on film, but his new paint job gives him a fresh look; it's also a nod to the Iron Man design from the *Ultimates* comics.

"Basically, I did several variations on the existing Mark 47, all in different ways to get a different graphical scheme. And the one that they gravitated toward and liked was the one based on *The Ultimates*."
— Concept Artist Phil Saunders

SAUNDERS

MEINERDING

FIFTH PERIOD

SCHOOL CLUBS

In addition to academics, Midtown's always had a variety of awesome organizations to join, and this year was no exception. In these clubs, we learned to work with our peers and sharpen our problem-solving skills—focusing on exploration, programming, and structures. No place is too far, no structure is too high, and no task is too big that we can't overcome i!

> "One of the ideas that always excited us is that heights are scary. This Spider-Man isn't irrationally afraid of heights, but afraid of being high off the ground the way any normal person like you or me would be. So when the writers of the first draft, Jonathan Goldstein and John Francis Daley, pitched us the concept of Spider-Man having to climb the Washington Monument—which is not only really tall, but there is nothing to web onto around it if he falls or gets into trouble—this just felt like a great way of making the audience fear for Peter's safety."
>
> **— Co-Producer Eric Carroll**

FRANCISCO

TAMM

Department of DAMAGE CONTROL

"In the comics, there's Damage Control, which is the cleanup crew that shows up after the super heroes blow up a bunch of buildings. And I love that idea. We're doubling down on this idea of all this weird super-hero, Dark Elf, crazy Hydra tech that exists in broken bits and pieces all over the world. We wanted to use Damage Control as the main hub of collecting that stuff—but not as this amazing, perfectly managed Nick Fury/S.H.I.E.L.D. operation. It's a lot more bureaucratic. There's lots of holes where things can fall through. You know, it's just a day job, except you're cleaning up remnants from a Hydra battle."

— Director Jon Watts

PUI

PUI

TAMM

MEINERDING

RUBIN

"The idea of seeing inside the suit, and seeing Peter and Ned try to hack it—and thinking of it as essentially a skintight Iron Man suit that has so much technology in it that unlocking it actually means you are unlocking skills and powers—is a pretty cool thing."
- Head of Visual Development Ryan Meinerding

PREVIOUS **KUNITAKE**

RUBIN

"We started with some existing high-end briefcases, and ultimately settled on a size and design that wasn't available off the shelf. This meant we had to make it, so we turned to Special Effects Supervisor Dan Sudick to build it. The trick was to have it unfold in a cool but believable way. This was done as a combination of several different foldable cases, and Visual Effects captured all the elements to give it motion."
— Property Master Kirk Corwin

MEINERDING

DECATHLON TRIP

WASHINGTON, D.C.

Ned

"Having a fear of heights is a common vulnerability to have—but combined with the ability to launch himself between buildings and the desire to protect humanity, Peter is faced with a constant question of who he is and what he stands for. We find him nervously scaling the Washington Monument, clutching railings, and hesitating before big leaps—but he always chooses to face these terrifying obstacles. Giving him a fear of the very thing he is uniquely able to do was an opportunity to demonstrate what kind of character he is. Plus, it's hilarious."

—Executive Producer and Vice President of Marvel Studios Louis D'Esposito

"We really loved the idea of a set piece where Peter would save his friends. So many of these big super-hero movies focus on heroes saving civilians. To have Peter need to save the girl that he has a crush on and the bully that always makes fun of him and his best friend sounded like a really fun way to put the pressure on Peter."

— Executive Producer Jeremy Latcham

172 **RUBIN,** 173 TOP **MEINERDING,** 173 BOTTOM **PUI**

MANDRADJIEV

MEINERDING

RUBIN

PREVIOUS **NIZZI**

NIZZI

RUBIN

RUBIN

RUBIN

PUI

NIZZI

SIXTH PERIOD

PHYSICAL EDUCATION

We work hard to train our brains, but can't forget about the rest of our bodies! Midtown students put their physicality to the test this year. We experienced new challenges that measured our hand-eye coordination, reflexes, agility, and overall physical fitness—not to mention our mental toughness—and learned to rely on the strength we already had within ourselves!

> "One of the ideas that came up was putting Peter on the Staten Island Ferry in some sort of disaster where the ferry gets split in half, and Spider-Man has to use all the abilities he's been practicing and all the cool new tech in his suit he's unlocked to deal with it. So we pitched it, expecting to hear it'd have to be 100 percent digital, but that wasn't the case. After talking to our amazingly talented department heads and their crews, they not only told us it was feasible, but everyone got really excited about actually building it. So while the sequence obviously involved a lot of work from our Visual Effects team, having that massive set—which actually moved and cracked apart—really helped the actors, stunt people, and extras, and gave the sequence an incredible sense of scale and danger."
>
> **— Co-Producer Eric Carroll**

LEUNG

BUOEN

LEUNG

One of the goals of *Spider-Man: Homecoming* was to push Peter's mental acuity and physical abilities to their limits in ways not yet seen on film. During one planning session, the filmmakers brainstormed a massive sequence they later learned would test the crew's ingenuity and physicality as well.

'We actually got some models of the ferry to put on the conference table, and the team took a look and discussed what it would take to achieve a practical look. What time, money, and all that would make sense? When we were discussing this sequence, we also didn't know if we would get permission to shoot on a real ferry, so we also had to build most of the ship in order to actually shoot parts of the sequence—not just for the physical action of ripping apart the ferry.'

— Production Designer Oliver Scholl

PREVIOUS **LEUNG**

LEUNG

FUENTEBELLA

Staten
CITY OF

"The idea was that there are these large drone pods that can fly out to an area and shoot out mini repulsor drones, and then those mini drones would attach onto whatever and then ignite. Like the one for the Hulkbuster [in Avengers: Age of Ultron] providing him with extra parts. I like the idea that Iron Man has these drones that follow him to do other stuff."
– Concept Artist Josh Nizzi

NIZZI 190–191 **TAMM,** 192–193 **FUENTEBELLA**

Staten Island Ferry

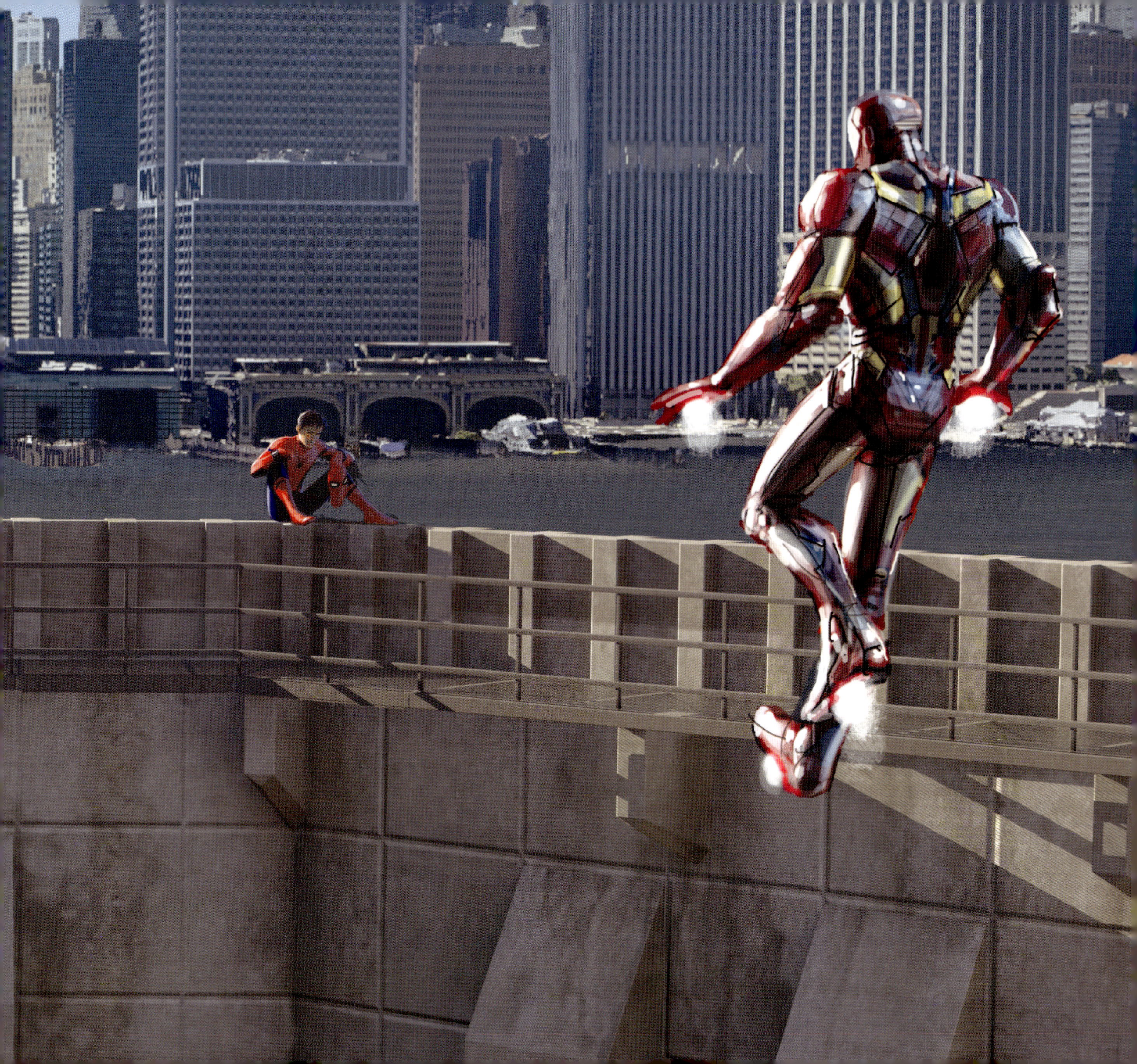

It's easy to get in over your head when you're still testing your limits and learning how your decisions can affect others. For Spider-Man, a bad situation could have ended much worse if not for Iron Man's help.

"Kids do stupid things. They go too fast. They don't stop and think. And to have that kind of attitude to the extent that Tony Stark has to say, 'Whoa, whoa, whoa—you gotta stop and think.' That's not something Tony Stark's used to saying. He's usually the rash one that's off making crazy decisions. To see Peter Parker put him in that position and kind of force Tony into a bit of a mentor role, or a fathering role, that's kind of fun. Especially because Tony Stark doesn't have kids. So seeing that dichotomy and seeing that relationship evolve is going to be super fun to put on film."

— Executive Producer Jeremy Latcham

PREVIOUS **RUBIN**

TAMM

HOMECOMING DANCE

It was a "Starry Night" for our Homecoming bash. The Dance Committee transformed our gym into a fabulous, beautifully decorated space where we could have fun and forget about our troubles. After weeks of anticipation, the big event lived up to the hype. It was truly A NIGHT TO REMEMBER!

> "Spider-Man has shown up to the homecoming dance and is realizing now he's going to have to choose between everything he's always wanted—including going to the dance with his dream girl—and stopping this really dangerous guy. Unfortunately, going after this guy pretty much guarantees he'll upset this amazing girl he's wanted to go on a date with for so long. It's a great moment, and really gets to that classic Spider-Man dilemma of trying to balance being a hero with everything that makes being a teenager in high school so hard."
>
> **— Co-Producer Eric Carroll**

BUOEN

BUOEN

PUI

School dances are a rite of passage defined by the excitement leading up to event, and the fun (or tears) that come afterwards. For most, those teenage moments are easy to recall, but Production Designer Oliver Scholl had to find inspiration for the film's dance in other ways.

"It's kind of funny, as I'm not from the United States. I grew up in Germany, so we didn't have this kind of stuff. It was interesting to hear these memories from Jon [Watts] himself and from my decorators who had these experiences. I tapped into their memories in what we saw. What we liked most were the layers of light and the strings and stars. It seemed very aspirational."

— Production Designer Oliver Scholl

MEINERDING

TOTALLY

23.30

INTERNATIONAL

PREVIOUS **LEUNG**

BUOEN

DETENTION

As we get older, our black-and-white world begins to fade into shades of gray. We learn life is not always as straightforward as we want it to be, and the right decision is not always the easiest. While we may stumble sometimes, our teachers try to instill within us an unwavering conviction not only to be better students, but also better human beings.

> "A big part of this movie is Peter growing into Spider-Man. He is still learning, he is still new to this, but we all know he will become one of the greatest heroes ever. We really wanted a final confrontation that didn't just provide amazing spectacle, but also reinforced this theme of him growing into his role—and realizing being a hero is hard and scary, not just glamour and fame. Earlier in the film, we see him struggle with climbing the Washington Monument, which he finds very frightening, and now here he is on the outside of a crashing plane that is more or less invisible—he doesn't know how he is going to stop the Vulture, or get back to the ground safely, so he has to learn to trust himself and figure things out in the moment. On top of that, he is grappling with the realization that the Vulture can be this dangerous criminal, but also a responsible family man—which throws him for a loop. It makes for this nuanced, emotional lesson that Peter has to overcome in the middle of this incredible fight!"
>
> **— Co-Producer Eric Carroll**

MEINERDING

"I really like tense thriller scenes, and I like very clear stakes in a movie even if it is just very, very simple. I like it when the audience knows exactly what has to happen, and they're just really worried that it's not going to."
— Director Jon Watts

"There is the great moment where the Vulture gets the upper hand and drops a warehouse on Spider-Man, trapping him. It seems like it's hopeless. The weight is just too much for this poor kid, and he can't budge it—which comes straight out of the comics, Amazing Spider-Man #33—and Spider-Man knows if he doesn't get out of there, lots of bad things will happen to a lot of good people. After panicking a bit, he realizes he doesn't need help, he doesn't need Iron Man to save him. He finds the strength within himself to lift off the tons of concrete and steel on top of him so he can go stop the Vulture."
– Eric Carroll

210–213 **TAMM**

TAMM

MEINERDING

MEINERDING

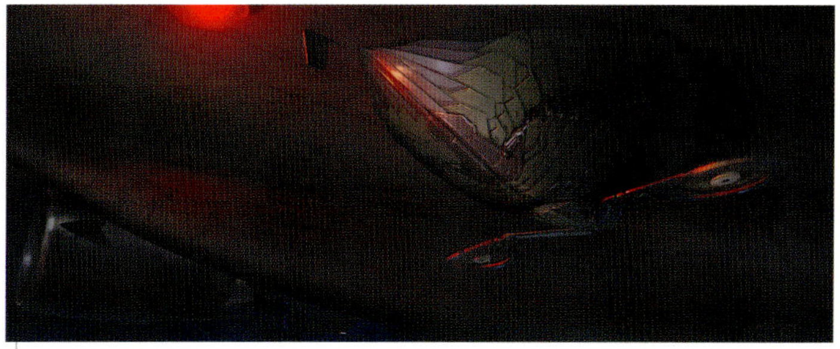

SAUNDERS

SAUNDERS

RUBIN | PREVIOUS MEINERDING

0339
04899
0338

70

In the film's tense final scenes, Spider-Man finds himself dangling from a single web-line high above New York City in pursuit of the Vulture, a villain unlike any he has encountered.

"The Vulture is almost a force of nature. He has more tech and is the type of opponent that Spider-Man has never faced before. But even with all that, we wanted to make it feel like Spidey can still overcome without the suit that Tony Stark made him give up. He is still Spider-Man without all of the gadgets—they don't define him."
— Concept Artist Rodney Fuentebella

MANDRADJIEV | TAMM

222–223 **MEINERDING,** 223 **FUENTEBELLA**

TAMM

FUENTEBELLA

"For most audiences, Peter Parker is the most relatable super hero in the MCU. He is flawed, he makes mistakes, but at the core of that is this deeply kind, charismatic young man who just wants to do the right thing. Peter finds himself possessing super-powers while still a high schooler negotiating his outward identity. Beyond that, he is the only character in the MCU who must keep this identity a secret. There is something so infectious about a character that is smart enough to concoct his own webbing, strong enough to fight an Avenger, and charming enough to win the affection of the prettiest girl in school. We took great care in casting someone who could portray those layers authentically, and Tom Holland does just that. He is the perfect Spider-Man both in and out of the suit."

- Executive Producer and Marvel Studios Co-President Louis D'Esposito

PUI

226–235 **MANDRADJIEV,**
238–239 **FUENTEBELLA**

PERCEPTION NYC

ART CLASS

While Midtown High is known primarily as a science and technology school, the arts are highly valued and considered an important part of the curriculum. Our students created some amazing pieces this year, and we've chosen to display some of our favorites here. Even though art is subjective, which do you like best? I'm partial to the one with Spider-Man! ;)

"When this started out, we were contacted by [Director] Jon Watts and [Executive Producer] Jeremy Latcham, who effectively said, 'We want something that is handmade and feels like a high-school art project.' And from there, we just ran with it. We explored two different components for this: One was figuring out what kinds of mediums would be appropriate for this; the other was figuring out what kinds of scenes we could present to show a combination of imagery that feels iconic to Spider-Man, as well as little ideas that help continue the story—particularly in terms of Spider-Man returning to Queens and being your friendly neighborhood Spider-Man to get into more playful, quirky, and simpler crimefighting tasks.

— Perception NYC Principal and Chief Creative John LePore"

PERCEPTION NYC

Every MCU fan knows to stay until the credits end for a scene teasing the next Marvel Studios film. But with *Spider-Man: Homecoming*, there's another reason to remain seated: the main-on-end title sequence created by Perception NYC. Featuring a series of vignettes using a variety of mixed-media imagery, the sequence is fun, energetic, and lighthearted—the perfect way to both begin the end credits and close out the film.

"The process here has been an incredible amount of fun. Our team on an average project spends the majority of the time working on a computer, and this was an opportunity for everybody to tap into an area of their brain that they don't use on a typical project. We've been doing a lot of work actually painting materials on paper, sculpting things out of children's sculpting clay, playing with more physical materials than we ever have had the opportunity to get our hands on. And that's something that has everybody eager to jump in."
-John LePore

PERCEPTION NYC

PERCEPTION NYC

Creating a nontraditional main-on-end sequence also meant using unconventional methods to build it. Even though Perception NYC was working with different mediums to shape the look of the sequence, the team made sure to maintain a sense of cohesiveness by tying all the shots together using various hues, tints, and shades.

"We didn't want to retell the movie. It's easy to kind of go back and do a recap of it visually. That's not what this sequence is about at all. There are certainly moments that touch on things that have happened, but it is by no means a summary of the film. We really wanted to create this dynamic, constantly changing, and unpredictable sequence."
-Perception NYC Co-Founder Jeremy Lasky

"We're being very mindful to use color as one of our few unifying aspects, because the mediums can have such different texture and even composition from each other. We wanted to have color be something that ties everything together, as well as a very casual approach to the aesthetic. We constantly refer to it as a high-school student who has slapped together his art project 15 minutes before class, and although we're obsessing over every little detail, we're working really hard to make sure that everything feels very spontaneous."
-John LePore

AFTERWORD 2017

Filmmaking is a collaborative process, and all the incredible talents I get to work with always instill in me a sense of gratitude. But there's an additional feeling of owing a group of people something profound. I really want to acknowledge all of the amazing artists that have brought Spidey to life for the past 55 years. There's a reason we have an extreme sense of nostalgia for this character, and for me it's mostly due to an incredibly talented group of artists that made Spider-Man the greatest super hero of all time.

Steve Ditko, John Romita Sr., Mike Zeck, John Buscema, Ron Frenz, Joe Quesada, Humberto Ramos, Paolo Rivera, J. Scott Campbell, Todd McFarlane, Erik Larsen, Mark Bagley, Sara Pichelli, Olivier Coipel, Adi Granov, Gabriele Dell'Otto, E.J. Krisor, and, of course, Alex Ross are the main sources of inspiration for me. These people helped shape an incredible icon, one that I have loved since I was very small. They are the source of my love and nostalgia for this character, and pretty much the driving force for my passion for Spidey.

For me, it started with *Spider-Man and His Amazing Friends*. I had the Underoos. I had the beach towel and countless action figures—including the one that slid down a string to simulate web-swinging. I watched every episode of the '90s animated series, and then fell in love with the McFarlane Spider-Man all over again. And then Alex Ross came along and showed us what the definition of "classic" Spidey really was. The Sam Raimi Spider-Man movies brought him to life in such a wonderful way; they are the gold standard of super-hero cinema.

So fast-forward a couple decades, and Kevin Feige walked into my office and casually said, "We have to do some designs for Peter." I looked up at him quizzically until he finished the sentence. "Parker." I think there was an audible gasp—or something like a gasp—and I might've blacked out for a second.

The first thing that popped into my head was: Romita. I Love with a capital "L" the licensing art John Romita Sr. did for Spidey. All of those poses are burned into my skull—and the head design is perfect. It was so solidly drawn, even with the flourishes in the eyes that most artists don't try to replicate. To me, that Spider-Man head is the logo of Marvel as much as Mickey Mouse is Disney's. The other two elements I love from Mr. Romita's Spidey are the small spider on the chest and the simple web design throughout the body. It feels like an innocent version of Spider-Man, one perfect for a younger Peter Parker.

Getting a whole suit design approved is sometimes a long journey. This one was a bit long. I am proud to say, however, the first and only head I did was approved on the first try—my closest approximation of a Romita Sr. Spider-Man head. Luckily Kevin, the Russo brothers and Jon Watts liked my idea of the emotive eyes, and the rest eventually fell into place. The other pieces of the puzzle were realizing that Tony Stark had designed it, and trying to integrate some elements from other MCU designs that Tony had built. And, of course, doing a more tech-based spider emblem.

I'm lucky in getting to write this afterword because I get to thank everyone that made this version of Spidey great. In this case, it starts with Kevin Feige, Tom Rothman, Amy Pascal, Louis D'Esposito, Victoria Alonso, Jeremy Latcham, Nate Moore, and Eric Carroll. Thank you all for letting me work on my favorite character. And thank you, Kevin, for keeping me around since Iron Man—there are no words to fully express how grateful I am. Next up, thanks to the Russo brothers and Jon Watts for trusting me to help figure out a new visual for an amazing icon, and thank you for doing him such amazing justice in your movies. Thank you to Judianna Makovsky, Louise Frogley, Robyn Gebhart, and their respective teams, who brought the practical costumes into reality, and to Dan DeLeeuw and Janek Sirrs for breathing life into their digital counterparts. Thank you to my team of Amazing artists—you guys did a Spectacular job on this one. Rodney, Phil, Josh, Josh, Alex, Iain, Paul, and Adam: You guys are superstars. And thank you to Jacob, AJ, and Bojan for keeping the machine running.

And finally, thank you to all of the amazing comic-book artists that have brought Spider-Man to life over the years. You have inspired so many True Believers, me included!

RYAN MEINERDING

CONTRIBUTOR BIOS 2017

DIRECTOR JON WATTS was born and raised in Fountain, Colorado, and studied film at New York University. He began his career directing music videos for artists including TV on the Radio and Fatboy Slim, as well as comedy sketches for *The Onion News Network*. His first film, *Clown*, was the result of a fake trailer that went viral. His next film, *Cop Car*, was shot in his hometown on a budget of $800,000. It premiered at Sundance Film Festival in 2015 to critical acclaim. He lives in Los Angeles with his wife, Dianne, and his dog, Donut.

Over the past decade, **PRODUCER AND MARVEL STUDIOS PRESIDENT KEVIN FEIGE** has played an instrumental role in a string of blockbuster feature films adapted from the pages of Marvel comic books. In his current role, Feige oversees all creative aspects of the company's feature film and home entertainment activities. He is currently producing *Spider-Man: Homecoming* and *Thor: Ragnarok*, which will hit theaters in 2017; *Black Panther, Avengers: Infinity War*, and *Ant-Man and the Wasp*, which will be released in 2018; and *Captain Marvel* and the fourth *Avengers* film, which will be in theaters in 2019. Earlier this year, he produced *Guardians of the Galaxy Vol. 2*. In 2016, Feige produced *Captain America: Civil War*, which crossed $1 billion in global box office and was the year's highest-grossing film, and *Doctor Strange*, which grossed more than $600 million worldwide. His previous producing credits for Marvel include *Iron Man 3, Marvel's The Avengers, Ant-Man, Avengers: Age of Ultron, Guardians of the Galaxy, Captain America: The Winter Soldier, Thor: The Dark World, Thor, Captain America: The First Avenger, Iron Man 2*, and *Iron Man*.

PRODUCER AMY PASCAL is the founder and CEO of Pascal Pictures, a film and television production company based at Sony Pictures Entertainment. In addition to the upcoming release of *Spider-Man: Homecoming*, Pascal's impressive slate of upcoming films includes a film adaptation of Molly Bloom's underground-poker memoir *Molly's Game*, written and directed by Aaron Sorkin, marking his feature directorial debut; a Steven Spielberg project based on the life of Katharine Graham, starring Meryl Streep and Tom Hanks; an animated Spider-Man film to be released in 2018; *The Girl in the Spider's Web*, the sequel to Stieg Larsson's successful *The Girl with the Dragon Tattoo* trilogy; and the live-action adaptation *Barbie*, based on Mattel's iconic fashion doll. Pascal grew up in Los Angeles, where she still resides with her husband and son.

CO-PRODUCER RACHEL O'CONNOR is the president of film and television at Pascal Pictures, a production company based at Sony Pictures Entertainment. In addition to being a co-producer on *Spider-Man: Homecoming*, O'Connor has been instrumental in developing Pascal Pictures' impressive slate, which includes the live-action adaptation *Barbie* based on Mattel's iconic fashion doll; an adaptation of the Pulitzer Prize-winning book *Blood in the Water*, to be directed by Christopher McQuarrie; and an original science-fiction project by writer/director Rupert Wyatt. Before making the move to Pascal Pictures, O'Connor worked as an executive at Sony for over 15 years. O'Connor was born and raised in Los Angeles, where she resides with her husband and son.

EXECUTIVE PRODUCER AND MARVEL STUDIOS CO-PRESIDENT LOUIS D'ESPOSITO served as executive producer on the blockbuster hits *Iron Man, Iron Man 2, Thor, Captain America: The First Avenger, Marvel's The Avengers, Iron Man 3, Thor: The Dark World, Captain America: The Winter Soldier, Guardians of the Galaxy*, and most recently *Captain America: Civil War, Avengers: Age of Ultron, Ant-Man, Doctor Strange*, and *Guardians of the Galaxy Vol. 2*. He is currently working on the highly anticipated films *Spider-Man: Homecoming, Thor: Ragnarok, Black Panther, Ant-Man and the Wasp, Captain Marvel*, and *Avengers: Infinity War*, as well as collaborating with Marvel Studios President Kevin Feige to build the future Marvel slate. As co-president of the studio and executive producer on all Marvel films, D'Esposito balances running the studio with overseeing each film from its development stage to distribution. In addition to executive-producing Marvel Studios' films, D'Esposito directed the Marvel One-Shot *Item 47*, which made its debut to fans at the 2012 San Diego Comic-Con International and was featured again at the LA Shorts Fest in September 2012. The project was released as an added feature on hte *Marvel's The Avengers* Blu-ray disc. D'Esposito also directed the second Marvel One-Shot *Agent Carter*, starring Hayley Atwell, which premiered at the 2013 San Diego Comic-Con to critical praise from press and fans, and is an added feature on the *Iron Man 3* Blu-ray disc. The One-Shot's popularity led to development of the TV series *Marvel's Agent Carter*. D'Esposito began his tenure at Marvel Studios in 2006. Prior to Marvel, D'Esposito's executive-producing credits include the 2006 hit film *The Pursuit of Happyness*, starring Will Smith; *Zathura: A Space Adventure*; and the 2003 hit *S.W.A.T.*, starring Samuel L. Jackson and Colin Farrell.

Marvel Studios **EXECUTIVE VICE PRESIDENT OF PHYSICAL PRODUCTION VICTORIA ALONSO** is executive-producing Jon Watts' *Spider-Man: Homecoming* and Taika Waititi's *Thor: Ragnarok*. In her executive role, she oversees postproduction and visual effects for the studio slate. She executive-produced James Gunn's *Guardians of the Galaxy Vol. 2*, Scott Derrickson's *Doctor Strange*, Joe and Anthony Russo's *Captain America: Civil War*, Peyton Reed's *Ant-Man*, Joss Whedon's *Avengers: Age of Ultron*, James Gunn's *Guardians of the Galaxy*, Joe and Anthony Russo's *Captain America: The Winter Soldier*, Alan Taylor's *Thor: The Dark World*, Shane Black's *Iron Man 3*, and Joss Whedon's *Marvel's The Avengers*. She co-produced Jon Favreau's *Iron Man* and *Iron Man 2*, Kenneth Branagh's *Thor*, and Joe Johnston's *Captain America: The First Avenger*. Alonso's career began at the nascency of the visual-effects industry, when she served as a commercial VFX producer. From there, she VFX-produced numerous feature films, working with such directors as Ridley Scott (*Kingdom of Heaven*), Tim Burton (*Big Fish*), and Andrew Adamson (*Shrek*), to name a few. Throughout the years, her dedication to the industry has been admired and her achievements recognized. In 2015, Alonso was an honoree of the New York Women in Film & Television's Muse Award for Outstanding Vision and Achievement. In January 2017, she received the Advanced Imaging Society's Harold Lloyd Award.

EXECUTIVE PRODUCER JEREMY LATCHAM is the senior vice president of production and development at Marvel Studios. He most recently served as an executive producer alongside writer/director Joss Whedon on Marvel's *Avengers: Age of Ultron*, the 2015 sequel to *Marvel's The Avengers*. Latcham also served as an executive producer on the latter film, as well as the blockbuster hit *Guardians of the Galaxy*. Latcham was associate producer on the critically acclaimed 2008 blockbuster *Iron Man*, and co-producer on the hit 2010 follow-up *Iron Man 2*. A graduate of Northwestern University, Latcham began his career at Miramax and Dimension Films, also working at the Endeavor Agency. He joined Marvel Studios in 2004, and has held the titles of vice president, director of development, and creative executive. In 2011, Variety featured Latcham as one of Hollywood's New Leaders.

PRODUCER PATRICIA WHITCHER's Marvel adventure began with *Thor* in 2011 and has continued with *Marvel's The Avengers, Avengers: Age of Ultron, Captain America: Civil War*, and *Spider-Man: Homecoming*. Next up is the highly anticipated *Captain Marvel*, Marvel's first film centered around a female super hero starring Brie Larson. Whitcher also served as executive producer on the reboot of *Godzilla* and other memorable films including *Dreamgirls, Memoirs of a Geisha, The Terminal*, and *My Best Friend's Wedding*. A lifelong Los Angeles resident, she is a graduate of Loyola Marymount University and the mother of two children.

CO-PRODUCER ERIC H. CARROLL began his career at Marvel Studios in 2009. Carroll was hired by Kenneth Branagh as a researcher on *Thor*, transitioning into the position of creative executive while that film was in production. He went on to serve as the creative executive on Marvel's *Thor: The Dark World*, and co-produced both seasons of the *Marvel's Agent Carter* TV series. *Spider-Man: Homecoming* is the first feature he has overseen for the studio. An alumnus of Fordham University's College at Lincoln Center, Carroll previously worked for Martin Scorsese in New York City before moving to Los Angeles, where he lives with his wife, Alyson, and their son, Clark, as well as their two rescue pups, Wendy and Ursula.

CO-PRODUCER AND VICE PRESIDENT OF PHYSICAL PRODUCTION MITCH BELL started with Marvel Studios in 2010. He oversaw production and was associate producer on *Captain America: The First Avenger, Iron Man 3*, and *Captain America: The Winter Soldier*, as well as co-producer on *Avengers: Age of Ultron* and *Captain America: Civil War*. He recently finished shooting *Spider-Man: Homecoming* and is co-producing *Avengers: Infinity War* and *Avengers 4* back-to-back. Bell was executive producer on several Marvel One-Shots including *Item 47, Agent Carter*, and *All Hail the King*. Prior to joining Marvel Studios, he was a freelance production supervisor with over 20 years of experience in both features and television. Originally from Fort Collins, Colorado, Bell moved to Los Angeles in the early '90s and started his career as a production assistant at Imagine Films.

DIRECTOR OF PHOTOGRAPHY SALVATORE TOTINO began building his reputation as one of the finest commercial and music-video DOPs of his generation. Today, he has over 500 commercials on his résumé, having contributed to high-profile campaigns including Jack Daniels, Nike, Jaguar, the Gap, and H.I.S Jeans, winning a Clio Award for the latter. He has lit music videos for such celebrated bands as Radiohead, R.E.M., Bruce Springsteen, Soundgarden, U2, and more. Born and raised in Brooklyn, New York, Totino is a fixture on director Ron Howard's team. The duo have collaborated on films such as *The Missing, Cinderella Man, Frost/Nixon, The Dilemma, Made in America, The Da Vinci Code, Angels & Demons*, and *Inferno*. Totino's first feature film as director of photography came in 1998 when Oliver Stone hired him to work on his football drama *Any Given Sunday*. Since then, Totino has compiled an impressive list of credits including *Changing Lanes, People Like Us, Concussion*, and *Everest*.

PRODUCTION DESIGNER OLIVER SCHOLL created worlds for *Independence Day (ID4), The Time Machine, Edge of Tomorrow, Suicide Squad,* and others before joining Jon Watts' exploration of Peter Parker's friendly neighborhood. Scholl published immense cross-sections of spaceships early in his life, then worked as an illustrator in Germany, designing advertising art and science-fiction book covers. After studying industrial design, a job as a conceptual designer for Roland Emmerich's *Stargate* led him to stay in Los Angeles. Initially working as a conceptual artist, Scholl contributed artwork to Sony's *Spider-Man 3* and Marvel's *Iron Man,* among others, not daring to dream he one day would have the opportunity to design Spider Man's world himself. When he's not roaming the world on location for his latest feature-film assignment, Scholl lives in Los Angeles with his wife Jennifer, daughter Kathryn, and son Trevor.

COSTUME DESIGNER LOUISE FROGLEY designed the costumes for Craig Gillespie's *The Finest Hours* and Gary Ross' *Free State of Jones.* Her most recent work can be seen in the upcoming *Spider-Man: Homecoming,* and she is in production on Marvel Studios' *Ant-Man and the Wasp.* Frogley has collaborated with Steven Soderbergh on five of his films, receiving Costume Designers Guild Awards nominations for Excellence in Contemporary Film for both *Ocean's Thirteen* and *Traffic.* In 2006, Frogley's designs for George Clooney's *Good Night, and Good Luck* earned a Costume Designers Guild nomination for Excellence in Period Film. For her work on Stephen Gaghan's *Syriana*, she received the Guild's nomination for Excellence in Contemporary Film. Frogley has designed over 20 features—including Tony Scott's *Spy Game* and *Man on Fire*, Ron Shelton's *Bull Durham*, the James Bond film *Quantum of Solace*, Robert Zemeckis' *Flight*, and Angelina Jolie's *Unbroken.* Born in Britain, Frogley spent her childhood commuting from school in England to her family's home in Kenya. She has been based in Los Angeles for the past twenty years.

PROPERTY MASTER KIRK CORWIN has worked on a diverse range of films—from *Ghostbusters, Pirates of the Caribbean: On Stranger Tides,* and *Dreamgirls* to *Wayne's World* and *Wayne's World 2, The Hudsucker Proxy,* and *River's Edge.* Corwin learned problem-solving at an early age from his parents, both engineers, who gave him his love of physical objects and design. He has enjoyed the collaborative world of filmmaking, focusing the ideas of the production designer and director into finished props on set. Corwin lives in Glendale, California, with his wife, Susie, and a garage full of great stuff—or as she calls it, "junk."

VISUAL EFFECTS SUPERVISOR JANEK SIRRS came west in 1993 to help establish Los Angeles offices for the London-based VFX company The Computer Film Company. Since then, he has worked independently as a visual effects supervisor on such films as *I Am Legend* and *The Hunger Games: Catching Fire* with director Frances Lawrence, *Batman Begins* with Christopher Nolan, *The Big Lebowksi* with the Coen brothers, Marvel's *Iron Man 2* with Jon Favreau, *Terminator Genisys* with Alan Taylor, and *Marvel's The Avengers* with Joss Whedon. Sirrs won an Academy Award and a British Academy of Film and Television Arts Award for his work on *The Matrix* with the Wachowskis in 1999; he also has been nominated for Oscars for *Iron Man 2* and *Marvel's The Avengers*, and BAFTA Awards for *Batman Begins* and *Marvel's The Avengers.*

VISUAL EFFECTS PRODUCER DIANA GIORGIUTTI's experience in film and television spans 36 years and includes some of Hollywood's most respected films. She is the executive producer of features at Luma Pictures, overseeing all feature production across both Luma's Los Angeles and Melbourne facilities. Prior to *Spider-Man: Homecoming,* Giorgiutti was the visual effects producer on Marvel Studios' *Ant-Man, Thor,* and *Thor: The Dark World.* Other projects have included work as stereo producer on Marvel's *Captain America: The First Avenger* and visual effects producer on Baz Luhrmann's *Australia,* for which she won 2008's Best Visual Effects Golden Satellite Award. Previously, Giorgiutti worked as digital effects producer on the highly acclaimed *Matrix* trilogy with the Wachowskis and Joel Silver. *The Matrix* won the Academy Award for Best Visual Effects. Before making the move to Los Angeles, Giorgiutti was based in London; she began her career in Sydney, Australia.

HEAD OF VISUAL DEVELOPMENT RYAN MEINERDING has been active as a freelance concept artist and illustrator in the film business since 2005. Even early in his career, his work was already drawing the kinds of raves reserved for industry veterans. After earning a degree in industrial design from Notre Dame, he transitioned to Hollywood and worked on 2008's *Outlander.* He was hired at Marvel Studios for *Iron Man,* and after leaving briefly to do concept work for *Transformers: Revenge of the Fallen* and *Watchmen,* has been full-time ever since. While working on *Iron Man 2,* Meinerding contributed the design for the new Iron Man armor in the comic-book series *Invincible Iron Man.* He served as visual development co-supervisor on *Captain America: The First Avenger, Thor,* and *Marvel's The Avengers.* He then served as head of visual development on *Iron Man 3, Captain America: The Winter Soldier, Avengers: Age of Ultron, Captain America: Civil War, Doctor Strange, Black Panther,* and *Spider-Man: Homecoming.* He is currently working on *Avengers: Infinity War* and loving every minute of it.

VISUAL DEVELOPMENT ILLUSTRATOR PHIL SAUNDERS has been contributing his designs for characters, vehicles, environments, and props to feature films from nearly every major studio since 2001. His involvement with Marvel Studios began with the first *Iron Man* film, and has continued through almost every Marvel production that has featured the popular character. For the decade prior to his work in film, he was the creative director for computer-game developer Presto Studios, an automotive designer for Nissan Design International, and a freelance designer of location-based entertainment.

VISUAL DEVELOPMENT ILLUSTRATOR ALEXANDER MANDRADJIEV has spent over 13 years working in the motion-picture industry as a cinematic illustrator. He has worked on such films as *Black Swan, Lincoln, Edge of Tomorrow, Rise* and *Dawn of the Planet of the Apes, Philip K. Dick's Electric Dreams, X-Men: First Class, Doctor Strange, Spider-Man: Homecoming, Black Panther, Marvel's The Avengers,* and more. Mandradjiev is a member of the Art Directors Guild - Local 800 of the International Alliance of Theatrical and Stage Employees working in Los Angeles.

VISUAL DEVELOPMENT ILLUSTRATOR JOSH NIZZI graduated from the University of Illinois with a degree in graphic design. He spent the next nine years working in video games as an art director, concept artist, modeler, and animator on games like *Red Faction* and *Red Faction II,* and *The Punisher.* Since then, Nizzi has been an illustrator for feature films such as *Transformers: Revenge of the Fallen, Dark of the Moon, Age of Extinction,* and *The Last Knight; Captain America: Civil War,* and *Avengers: Age of Ultron.* Recently, he has been splitting his time between his own video-game projects and feature-film work.

NATIVIDAD

ACKNOWLEDGMENTS

Victoria Alonso
Alexis Auditore
Ramsey Avery
Jacob Batalon
Mitch Bell
Richard Buoen
Cantina Creative
Christian Cordella
Will Corona Pilgrim
Kirk Corwin
Louis D'Esposito
Matt Delmanowski
Erika Denton
Digital Domain
John Eaves
Kevin Feige
Anthony Francisco
Louise Frogley
Rodney Fuentebella
Diana Giorgiutti
Laura Harrier
Josh Herman
Eric Hauserman
Carroll
Tom Holland
Elissa Hunter
Iloura
Imageworks
Kevin Kalaba
Tani Kunitake
Ryan Lang
Phil Langone
Percival Lanuza
Jeremy Lasky
Jeremy Latcham
John LePore

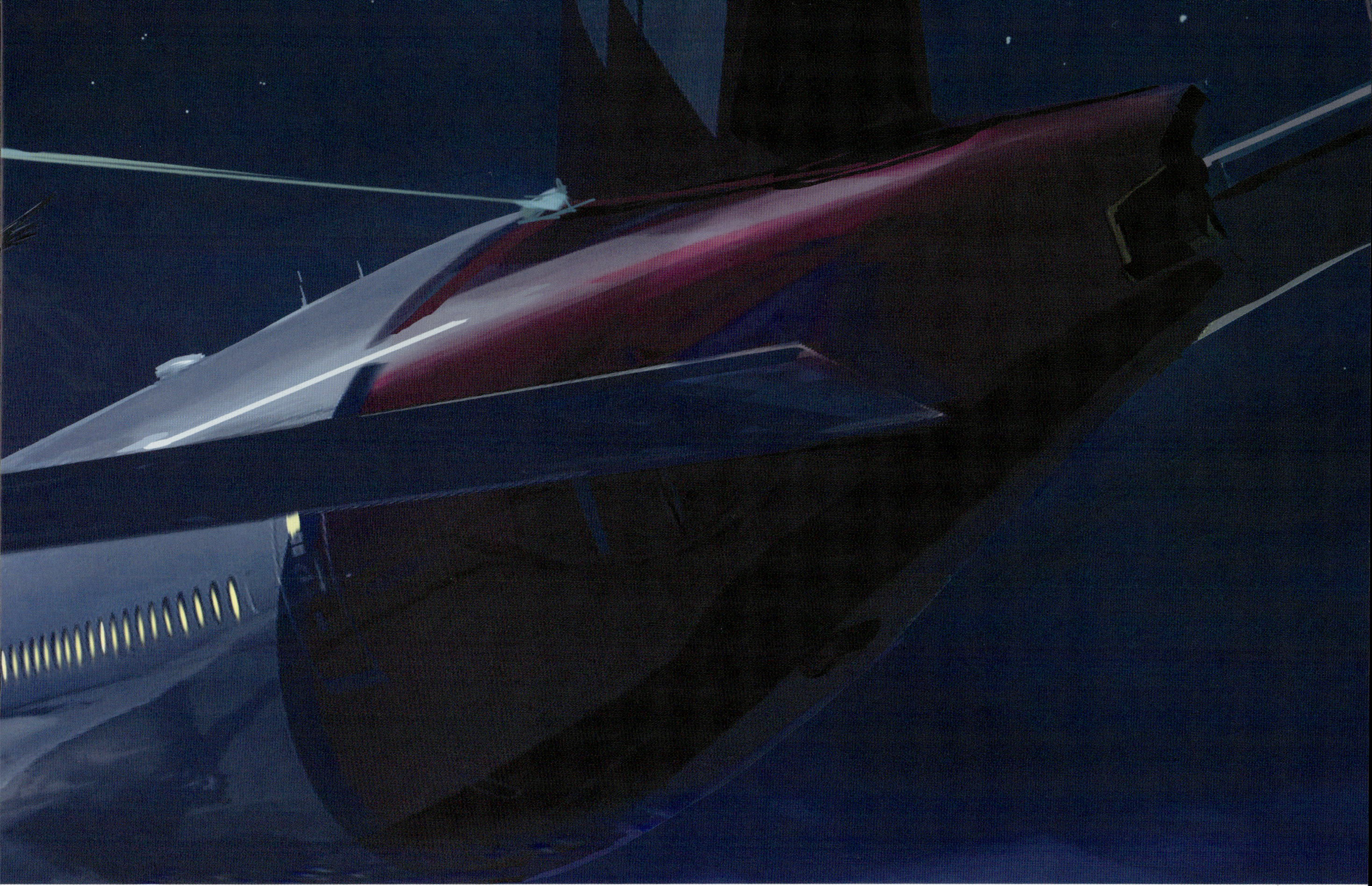

KUNITAKE

Andrew Leung
Luma Pictures
Alexander Mandradjiev
Randy McGowan
Ryan Meinerding
Method
Samuel Michlap
Ed Natividad
Josh Nizzi
Paul Ozzimo
Andy Park
Amy Pascal
Perception NYC
Avia Perez
Jacque Porte
Ryan Potter
Vicki Pui
Tony Revolori
Angourie Rice
Peter Rubin
Phil Saunders
Oliver Scholl
Janek Sirrs
Henrik Tamm
Salvatore Totino
Trixter
Jon Watts
Patricia Whitcher
Zendaya

ARTIST CREDITS

Ramsey Avery
Page 63

Richard K. Buoen
Pages 64, 184, 200-202, 206-207

Christian Cordella
Page 19

John Eaves
Pages 41, 68-73, 76, 80-81, 127, 135

Anthony Francisco
Page 165

Rodney Fuentebella
Pages 12-13, 32, 39, 43, 46-47, 50-53, 55, 74-75, 80-82, 93-94, 100-103, 114, 144-145, 184-185, 189, 192-193, 223, 237-239

Josh Herman
Pages 29, 105

Kevin Kalaba
Page 18

Tani Kunitake
Pages 16, 64-67, 74-75, 78-79, 168-169

Ryan Lang
Pages 30, 32

Phil Langone
Page 139

Andrew Leung
Pages 8-9, 184, 186-189, 204-205

Alexander Mandradjiev
Pages 54, 82-86, 91, 95, 132-133, 136-139, 142-143, 146-147, 174-175, 224-235

Ryan Meinerding
Dust jacket
Pages 20-28, 30-31, 33-40, 42, 44-45, 49, 57, 90, 92, 94, 111, 114, 118-120, 122-127, 129-131, 140-141, 148-157, 160-161, 170-171, 173, 176, 203, 280-209, 216-219, 221-223, 248-249, 254-255

Samuel Michlap
Page 60

Ed Natividad
Page 251

Josh Nizzi
Pages 48-49, 55-57, 77, 87-90, 94, 96-100, 103-104, 108-110, 112-113, 116-117, 177-179, 181, 194-195

Paul Ozzimo
Pages 104-107, 112, 115

Andy Park
Pages 10-13, 32

Perception NYC
Pages 2-3, 15-16, 162-163, 182-183, 242-247

Vicki Pui
Pages 16-17, 58-62, 127, 164-165, 167, 173, 180, 202, 240-241

Peter Rubin
Pages 170, 172, 176-177, 180, 196-197, 220-221

Phil Saunders
Pages 108, 113, 157-159, 221

Oliver Scholl
Page 127

Henrik Tamm
Pages 4-5, 16-17, 64-65, 120-121, 128-129, 134-135, 164-167, 190-191, 198-199, 210-215, 225, 236-237

MEINERDING

Autographs

Hey Peter, this year has been crazy!!! I still can't believe my best friend is Spider-Man!! Promise me you'll take me to the Avengers tower... that's all I ask (the mask thing doesn't count), just to gaze upon the glory of those heroes would be great. But anyway, I'll see you tonight because tonight is Star Wars and pizza night, and I'm really looking forward to seeing Darth Vader go all dark side on some rebels.

-Ned

P.S. what do you think about me possibly having a sidekick costume?

Have a good summer, See you next year! Cheer up.

-Betty

Hey Peter. Hope you're ready to dominate decathlon next year... we'll be going for back to back wins. Should be fun too.

-Michelle

Dear ________

You're welcome for knowing me.

From Spiderman's Best friend

Flash

Dear Peter-

This year has had its ups and downs, but I believe in you and know that your heart is in the right place.

Love,

Liz